HOW TO DISTILL

HOW TO DISTILL

A Complete Guide
from Still Design
and Fermentation
through Distilling
and Aging Spirits

AARON HYDE

HARVARD
COMMON
PRESS

Inspiring | Educating | Creating | Entertaining

Brimming with creative inspiration, how-to projects, and useful information to enrich your everyday life, quarto.com is a favorite destination for those pursuing their interests and passions.

First Published in 2022 by The Harvard Common Press, an imprint of The Quarto Group,
100 Cummings Center, Suite 265-D, Beverly, MA 01915, USA.
T (978) 282-9590 F (978) 283-2742 Quarto.com

The Harvard Common Press titles are also available at discount for retail, wholesale, promotional, and bulk purchase. For details, contact the Special Sales Manager by email at specialsales@quarto.com or by mail at The Quarto Group, Attn: Special Sales Manager, 100 Cummings Center, Suite 265-D, Beverly, MA 01915, USA.

26 25 24 23 22   3 4 5

ISBN: 978-1-55832-975-1

Digital edition published in 2022
eISBN: 978-1-55832-976-8

Library of Congress Cataloging-in-Publication Data available

Design: www.traffic-design.co.uk
Page Layout: Megan Jones Design
Photography: Fiona Goodall Photography and shutterstock
Front Cover Illustration: www.traffic-design.co.uk

Printed in China

CONTENTS

INTRODUCTION

This book has one goal and one goal only: to teach you how to distill! Whether you're completely new to the idea of distilling or have distilled a few times but want to learn more, I'm hoping this will get you going on your journey.

A lot of folks learn the art of distilling from a friend or family member. It's the kind of skill that is often handed down. For many, distilling was a natural progression from wine making or home brewing. Perhaps you took a different route though; maybe you're an avid whiskey collector who wanted to get your hands dirty and try distilling yourself, or maybe you found a still at an antiques shop or in your grandpappy's barn. No matter how you've gotten here, I'm glad to welcome you to distilling.

In this book, I'll try to keep distilling as simple as possible and focus on the practical. I will not rely on half-truths, folklore, hearsay, and will share only my opinion on a subject if I think it would be helpful. You may have noticed there's a lot of folklore and backcountry know-how when it comes to distilling. Some is grounded in technique while other parts are complete baloney. In many instances, you'll need to be cautious with information you find. On top of all this, the spirits industry has done a great job of creating mystique around their products. Learning the process of distilling in a straightforward manner will hopefully demystify both confusing secondhand information you may have picked up as well as the mystique of some marketing material from distilleries. I don't want to take away from spirits culture; rather I hope to enhance your appreciation of the craft and point the way towards quality.

Similar to hobbies like home brewing, you'll find distilling has both a science and artful components. I may not go into every detail found in scientific texts, but in this book I will highlight a bit of science when necessary—and when I think it's relevant to helping you get the best spirit possible. I'm also excited to share a taste of the artistic side of the hobby, from customizations to the art of tasting and blending.

Remember that this process isn't like paint by numbers! Creativity is what makes the hobby fun and rewarding. If the distilling process is understood and done well, given a bit of practice and continuous learning, your product will reflect what you put into it. While this book will provide the first steps and a pathway, I encourage you to deviate and experiment, within reason and keeping safety principles in mind. (Personal creativity is what makes whiskeys that are all made in a similar way, using similar ingredients and similar stills, even similar barrels, turn out so different.)

At its core distilling is a simple, beautiful process, and can be done quickly in the case of spirits like vodka and gin, or with years of patience and practice in the case of aged and blended whiskies and rums. I encourage you to read on, and as you go, jump right in and give this rewarding hobby a try!

QUESTIONS ABOUT THE LAW

There are few places in the world where home distilling is legal. I'm lucky to live in one of them right now, New Zealand. I'm from the United States where it is a federal crime, a felony, to make spirits for consumption. I know plenty of people who have home distilled in the United States, but that doesn't make it any more legal.

As with many things, there may be ways around the legality in your country, such as filing for a distilling license or permitting the still for use to make fuel. You won't find many places that allow you to make alcohol for consumption, even your own, even in your own home. It may seem antiquated since home brewing and wine making are legal in most of the world, but distilling has been deemed a different kettle of fish— sometimes under the guise of being a more dangerous process. In my opinion, it's no more dangerous than a hobby like woodworking if you take care and understand what you're doing.

In any case, get to know your local laws, and if you decide to take the risk, understand the penalties. Also, in no country is it legal to sell your homemade spirit without some sort of permit. We can't all live somewhere like New Zealand, but we can all be aware of what rules are in place locally, so take some time to understand what is legal and illegal to do in your country when it comes to distilling.

Beyond spirits, the process of distilling is actually used in many ways: to purify water, make oil products from petroleum, remove essential oils from flowers for perfume, to make ethanol fuel, and last but not least, to make spirits for consumption. The still you use and the techniques you learn can be used in some part to do all of the above.

BEFORE YOU BEGIN: THE DISTILLING PROCESS

In this book, the distilling process will be broken down into three to six basic steps you'll perform in the following order:

1. Mashing

2. Fermenting

3. Distilling

4. Polishing

5. Aging

6. Blending/Bottling

I'll cover all six of these steps, although all may not be necessary to create your chosen spirit. Can you pick out the three from this list you may not need depending on what spirit you're making?

The steps you may not always need are 1. Mashing, which is used for grains only; 4. Polishing, which is used to remove unwanted off flavors; and 5. Aging, which is used primarily for creating dark spirits. So, if you're looking to follow the easiest path, you can make a spirit like vodka or gin and follow just steps 2, 3, and 6!

My goal is to get you comfortably through all the steps you need to follow to make your chosen spirit. Moonshine? Yep. Gin? You bet. Bourbon? You can do it! Brandy? Let's make it. By the end of this book, you'll understand how to distill numerous different spirits and should have something coming out of your still that you can be proud to drink and share.

THE KEY STEPS AND NECESSARY EQUIPMENT

Each chapter of this book will delve deeper into its relevant topic and the standard equipment (minus grains, malts, and yeasts, and so on) you will need for each step, but this brief overview should help you as you begin your journey into making spirits.

STEP 1: MASHING (CHAPTER 1)

If you're already a home brewer, you know the mashing process is used on grains, which are sometimes referred to as cereals, to provide the brewer (or distiller) with simple sugars that can be eaten by yeast.

Many different spirits can be made using grain, including whiskey. However, if you're drinking something like vodka or gin, it probably is made from plant-based, naturally occurring sugars, as this is the cheapest route. These sugars don't need to be mashed, saving you the time and energy of the mashing step.

The equipment you will need for mashing includes the following:

- Long stainless steel spoon or mash paddle
- Pitcher for pouring water over grains
- Mash tun (at least 5 gallons or 19 liters)
- Sparge water heater (also known as a hot liquor tank)
- High-temperature silicone tubing
- Grain mill (optional)
- Heat source
- Water source

Left to right: Grainfather G30 with T500 copper reflux column, alembic still with copper column, T500 boiler with copper alembic dome and condenser, Still Spirits air still

STEP 2: FERMENTING (CHAPTER 2)

Turning sugar into alcohol is a critical step in the distilling process. While you can purchase wine, beer, or cider with the intent to distill it, these beverages were not made for distilling, so your results may vary. When you ferment your own alcohol, you have more control over the outcome. You will choose a yeast that is quite efficient at absorbing sugar and creating alcohol as a by-product. At times, you may choose a yeast to provide and emphasize particular flavors from the sugary product, while other times you may select a yeast to produce a clean, neutral flavor. Thus, by fermenting you are in the driver's seat during the creation of alcohol and the initial flavor development.

The equipment you will need for fermenting includes the following:

- Fermenter (at least 6 gallons, or 23 liters) with a lid
- Airlock
- Specific gravity hydrometer
- Racking cane with plastic tubing or autosiphon with plastic tubing (optional)

STEP 3: DISTILLING (CHAPTER 3)

The distilling process itself is that one step unique to making spirits (as opposed to making beer or wine), in that you are separating and concentrating the alcohol. Beer and wine usually aren't over 15 percent alcohol by volume (ABV) for a reason: They haven't been distilled. A typical beer these days is around 5 percent ABV, wine around 13 percent, and most spirits are around 40 percent (though liqueurs are often less).

In this book, I will assume you will use a still to do this, though there are other methods, such as freeze distillation. Still types will be covered in Chapter 10, but you've probably seen one online, at a home brew shop or maybe on a distillery tour. It has a boiler, a closed dome or column on the top for some amount of refluxing (re-condensing of vapor inside the still), and a condenser arm or tube that cools the vapor back to liquid form. The use of a still to perform distillation to concentrate alcohol is the only big difference between making spirits and making beer or wine.

The equipment you will need for distilling includes the following:

▸ Still (see Chapter 10)

▸ Proof and tralle hydrometer

▸ 12 to 15 collection jars (16 oz or 500 ml)

▸ Distiller's parrot or 250 ml glass test jar (cylinder)

▸ Water source

▸ Heat source

▸ Boil enhancers (optional)

STEP 4: POLISHING (CHAPTER 4)

If you're looking for a nice, clean, and neutral-flavored spirit postdistillation then polishing is the answer. This filtration step can improve your spirit by taking out impurities (created mostly during fermentation). If you're aging your spirit, a small amount of these flavors can be good! But if not, they can leave a pretty nasty off flavor and aroma in your clear spirit. If you're careful how you collect your alcohol, leaving the heads and tails separate, you can add these postdistillation in quantities that cut down on the nasty flavors, and maybe add some character to your spirit. Or, if you're making a whiskey that's going to be aged a long time, a polishing step can be less critical and maybe not even necessary.

The equipment you will need for polishing includes the following:

▸ Activated carbon

▸ Carbon filter

▸ Collection vessel

STEP 5: AGING (CHAPTER 5)

Aged or matured spirits are usually easy to identify. The yellow, amber, or brown color you see in spirits like whiskeys, rums, brandies, and tequilas comes from the aging process, usually from contact with toasted or charred oak or another type of wood. The burnt parts of the wood begin to color the spirit almost immediately and new bold and beautiful flavors like vanilla and caramel and tobacco will develop given time. At home, this can be done with charred oak chips, staves, or spirals in a glass jug or jar, or by putting your spirit directly in a small toasted or charred barrel.

The equipment you will need for aging includes the following:

▸ Toasted or charred oak barrel (minimum 2 gallons or 6 to 8 liters) or oak chips, staves, or cubes

▸ Muslin cloth (or coffee filters)

▸ Glass aging jug or vessels (if not using a barrel)

▸ Glass or stainless steel barrel thief or wine thief (for taking samples if using a barrel)

▸ Stainless steel racking cane and silicone tubing (for transfer if using a barrel)

▸ Stainless steel funnel

STEP 6: BLENDING AND BOTTLING (CHAPTER 6)

There are numerous things you can still do after distilling, polishing, and/or aging to improve your spirits. The first that comes to mind is blending. Part art, part science, the position of master blender is a position at many large whiskey makers that takes years of apprenticeship and experimentation, learning the common flavors and off flavors associated with distilling and aging—and really understanding your own palate. Honing your own sensory skills can be valuable to blending your own spirits.

Packaging your spirit in a properly corked, waxed, and labeled bottle may not be seen as critical by all in the distilling community, but it's a nice touch. True, maybe you'll decide your collection jug is the best final package for your particular spirit! However, the classic way to finish most spirits is a clear glass bottle (500 ml or 750 ml being common sizes), as a clear bottle offers a good look at the spirit itself.

The equipment you will need for blending and bottling include the following:

▸ Glass or stainless wine thief

▸ Assorted small glass test jars or beakers

▸ Journal or notes

▸ Tasting glass

▸ 100 to 250 ml graduated glass test jar for blending

▸ Spirit bottles of your choice

▸ Glass or stainless pitcher or autosiphon with silicone tubing (optional)

▸ Spirit bottle corks or caps

▸ Labels

If you haven't yet purchased your still and are unsure where to go from here, consider skipping ahead to Chapter 10 to learn more about still types and which to use for a particular spirit. A pot still will be the way to go if you're interested in whiskey, rum, or brandy; you'll want a column still for vodka and schnapps. It's possible to use either a pot or column still for gin. (Chapters 7 through 9 discuss these spirits and their variations and offer recipes for you to try.) A few other pieces that can be used throughout the process are necessary for particular spirits and if you want to make life easy. If you're unfamiliar with much of this equipment, start researching what's available, and read on to better understand how it will be used.

MASHING
Chapter 1

The first step in your distilling journey, if you choose to use grain, is mashing. If you're exclusively using agave, molasses, honey, dextrose, table sugar (sucrose,) or any other type of sugar, you can move right to the next chapter on fermentation, as your sugars are ready to be absorbed by yeast without mashing. A definite advantage to using preprocessed and naturally occurring simple sugars is that you don't have to mash, which can be one of the most complex steps in the entire distilling process.

Mashing is the process of converting starches, a complex carbohydrate, or complex sugar, into a simple carbohydrate, or simple sugar, like glucose. The larger sugar molecule is broken down into smaller sugar molecules by enzymes that occur in malt or are added during mashing. This is done with numerous types of malted and unmalted (raw) grains, all of which contain starches. Of those grains, barley is one of the most commonly used, and for many reasons: Barley's easy to malt; it's easy to mash; it tastes good; it grows in a variety of climates; and the list goes on.

Of course, other grains such as rye, wheat, rice, and oats show up in spirits quite often. They all contain starch and can be mashed from a complex sugar to more simple sugars. You may be familiar with the mandatory use of one such grain, corn (maize), in America's favorite style of whiskey, bourbon. Most grains are used close to home, where they grow well, and there's a lot of corn grown near bourbon distilleries. Climate and growing conditions in certain regions strongly influence what types of spirits become culturally significant to a country. Sorghum and rice go into the baijius of China, as they are grown locally. Outside of grain, grapes go into the cognacs of France. Considering the demand for grain-based spirits like whiskeys, baijius, and many famous gins and vodkas, grains are critical to making many of the most popular spirits in the world.

MASHING EQUIPMENT

When you're mashing, the goal is to steep grain in hot water and hold it at the right temperature (typically around 149°F or 65°C) for a long enough time (typically around sixty minutes) for the enzymes to activate and effectively convert the starch into simple sugar. Then you need to rinse and collect this sugar wash from the grain. This is called saccharification, the process of breaking down complex carbohydrates, like starch, into simple sugars.

If you already all-grain home brew, you'll probably have everything you need for mashing. If not, read on. Basic items to have around include

- Long (around 24 inches or 61 cm) stainless steel spoon or mash paddle
- 2-quart (2-liter) pitcher for pouring water over grains, or collecting wort
- Mash tun (at least 5 gallons or 19 liters in size, but larger is helpful)
- Sparge water heater (also known as a hot liquor tank)
- 3 feet (1 meter) of high-temperature silicone tubing
- Grain mill (optional)
- Wort chiller (optional)

Left to right: Grainfather counterflow chiller, Sparge water heater, mash paddle, water pitcher, and Grainfather G30 electric brewing system with mash basket

THE MASH TUN AND SPARGE WATER HEATER

The two big pieces of gear you'll need when mashing are a mash tun and sparge water heater. Mashing is typically done in a mash tun, a vessel designed to allow you to hold the temperature of your grain during mashing, allowing enzymes the right environment to convert starch into sugar. To hold temperature, it is usually well insulated or can be heated. It also allows you to separate your sugary wash, the liquid, from the grain. This means it typically has a false bottom, a flat screen that sits inside your vessel, providing a way for liquid to pass through a bottom valve but not through the grain. A bazooka screen, a tubular mesh screen thread into the inside of the ball valve, can achieve the same result. The goal at the end of mashing is separation of grain and liquid, so any well thought-out mesh material, like a nylon or cotton bag, or a perforated screen, to strain the grain will work.

A sparge water heater, or hot liquor tank (HLT) as it's also known, serves the important, albeit boring, purpose of heating water for rinsing your grains after mashing is complete. The objective is to rinse all of the sugar out of your mashed grains, so that the sugary liquid is separated from the grains for fermentation. For some mashes that require a large amount of rinsing water, the sparge water heater needs to be large enough to hold up to 6.5 gallons (25 liters) of water at 180°F (82°C). An 8-gallon (30-liter) stainless kettle will do the trick.

MOST COMMON MASH TUNS USED BY HOME BREWERS OR HOME DISTILLERS

STAINLESS KETTLE WITH FALSE BOTTOM. This is a simple and easy mash tun that can be gently heated to hold mash temperature.

STAINLESS KETTLE WITH STEEPING BAG. A large nylon bag is often used to steep and hold grains when mashing. This "brew in a bag" or "BIAB" method can be somewhat effective. Often the challenge here is effectively rinsing the grains of their sugar if rinsing is used at all (see No Sparge and Cold Sparge sidebar on page 20). Managing consistent temperatures inside the mash can also be a challenge, as applying heat to a mash kettle with a nylon bag can scorch or melt the bag, so be careful when using this method.

STAINLESS ELECTRIC KETTLE WITH PUMP AND FALSE BOTTOM. Numerous brewing systems are designed to mash with a pump. This recirculating infusion mash system (RIMS) will provide you with one of the most consistent methods for holding temperature as wort is recirculated from the heater to the top of the grain bed, allowing for an even temperature across the grain bed. ("Wort" is the name for your sugary wash while it's in the mash tun and before it's fermented, at which point it becomes "wash.")

INSULATED 5- OR 10-GALLON DRINK COOLER WITH FALSE BOTTOM. A traditional home brewing mash tun, the goal here is to close the mash in a well-insulated cooler so that the temperature remains consistent for an hour or so. Simple and effective.

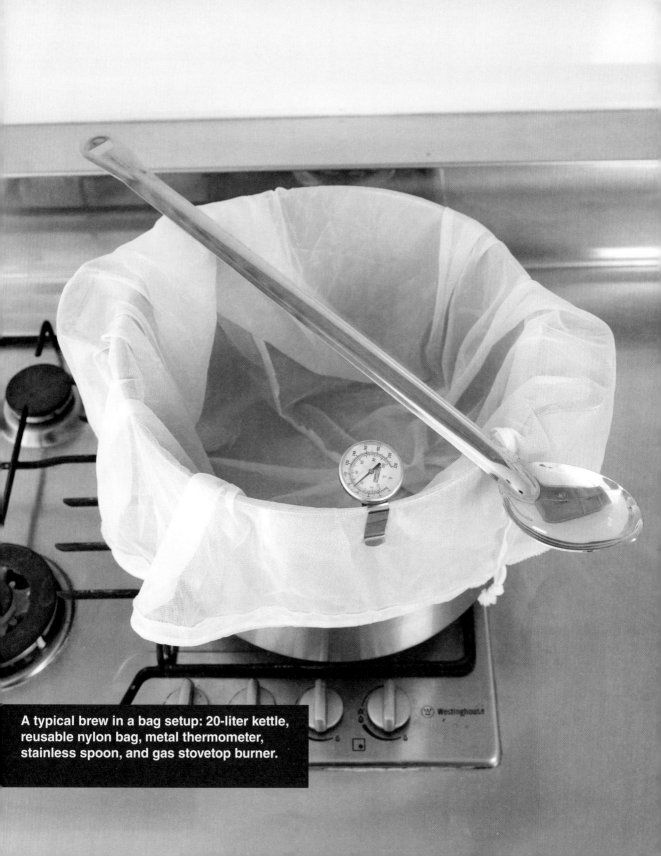

A typical brew in a bag setup: 20-liter kettle, reusable nylon bag, metal thermometer, stainless spoon, and gas stovetop burner.

NO SPARGE AND COLD SPARGE

No-sparge mashing is a popular technique in home brewing. It's also referred to as brew-in-a-bag mashing, as it's typically done in a large nylon bag that can be removed from the mash tun. It is occasionally used for home distilling, mostly in the thin mash process. The process eliminates the use of a sparge water heater vessel (most likely a kettle) and leaves you with only one vessel to manage when mashing. What you will need is a vessel that can manage your mash and sparge volume all in one spot, and either a mesh bag to steep and mash the grain that can be removed, or a mash vessel that can be drained, leaving behind the grain, the same as the traditional method discussed in this book.

One other consideration is "cold sparging" with cold to warm water, but not hot water. Instead of using water at 180°F (82°C), a higher temperature than your mash that denatures enzymes, cold sparging relies on simply pouring whatever water you have readily available over your mash to rinse it. Typically your tap water, it could just be cold water right from the kitchen sink. This technique is gaining favor with home brewers and distillers looking to simplify their process.

I often use this method with a standard water pitcher, collecting water from my faucet and pouring over the mash, usually when I'm in a hurry. One downside is that rinsing with cold to warm water may be less effective at rinsing the sugar from a mash, but only just slightly. Since you may not be boiling your mash water afterward, it does help bring your wash down to yeast pitching temperature faster. It's less popular in home brewing than in distilling because in brewing you want to deactivate the mash enzymes so they don't keep working and create too much simple sugar, whereas in distilling we want as much simple sugar as possible to convert into alcohol during fermentation. In brewing you're also raising the temperature after the mash to a boil.

Cold water can be an effective way to sparge if you don't have a second kettle or vessel to heat sparge water.

To use the cold sparging technique for the recipes in this book, simply ignore heating your sparge water up, using the volumes indicated in the recipe to rinse your grain with whatever temperature water you have on hand. If you're comfortable with slightly lower efficiency (less sugar creation, in the region of 2 to 10 percent) during your mash, trying either no sparge or cold sparge might be worth your while, as it can save both time and energy when mashing.

A variety of malted barley.

BARLEY MALT AND OTHER MALTED GRAIN

Folks in the industry might simply use the term "malt" to describe malted barley, as opposed to raw barley. Raw barley isn't easy to find in most places that cater to distillers, though you might find it as seed for planting or as feed for livestock. Because barley is the most popular malted grain in the world, it often gets shortened to just "malt." It can be confusing, I know, and it's a stumbling block for folks starting out when talking to a distiller friend or going online for information. Any other grain variety is typically mentioned in the name when referring to it as a malted product, like "wheat malt" or "rye malt."

Adding to this, based on the type of malting process used, the type of grain, the region, and numerous other factors, you'll hear a lot of different names for barley malt besides just malt. Here are the most common names and types of malted barley used in distilling, and as mentioned before, any of these might be referred to simply as malt:

▸ Distiller's malt

▸ Six-row malt

▸ Two-row malt

▸ Pale Ale malt

▸ Base malt

▸ Brewer's malt

▸ Ale malt

Mashing malted grain is the typical process used in making many whiskeys, but also in numerous other spirits. Using malted grain provides many benefits to you, the distiller.

1. **Storage.** Malted grains, if stored in a cool, dry place can last upward of two years, possibly even longer. Raw grains have a high moisture content and can mold or rot easily if not dried properly.

2. **Starch Access.** The starch inside is powdery from the dehydration from malting, and the husk or hull on the outside is easily cracked open. With a bit of water, this starch mixes and dissolves easily into hot water during mashing.

3. **Enzyme Access.** Barley and many other grains contain enzymes they'd typically use for plant growth. When malted, these enzymes become accessible, and we use them to convert starches into sugars during mashing.

4. **Flavor.** Malted barley has technically been cooked (or "kilned," as a maltster would refer to it), which adds some flavor to the grain. A variety of kilning and roasting types can be done, creating unique malt flavors you should challenge yourself to experiment with on your distilling journey.

5. **Mashing Filtration/Separation.** The husk of malted barley is no longer as soft as it was when it was harvested and maintains its structure when cracked open. When mashing we'll need to rinse the sugar from the grain and having malted barley husks in a mash make it much easier to rinse, filter, and collect the sugar. Some grains, like rye, don't have a husk and won't provide this nice filtration. This makes straining, rinsing, and washing sugar from the mash tun much more difficult, unless you add husks or hulls from other grains (often oats or rice) into the mash tun.

Peat being harvested from a bog.

PEATED MALT

Peat is decayed plant material that has formed in bogs and wetlands over many thousands of years. The type of peat that forms depends on the plants, such as grass or moss, in the area and the location of the peat bog. This location from which the peat is obtained, whether seaside or inland, is said to strongly affect the smoky flavor of the spirit produced.

Peated malt, or just peat malt, has a distinctive, smoky flavor and is used to make Scotch whiskeys, most notably those distilled on the island of Islay. Peat was used as fuel long ago. Now, when making peated malt, the peat is burned during the early stages of kilning, when the recently germinated (or green) malt's moisture is being reduced from around 45 percent to around 20 percent. At this stage, the malt can most easily absorb peat smoke flavor compounds. In this way, peat is no longer burned as a heat source as it historically once was, the by-product being a smoky flavored malt. Now it is simply burned as a source of flavor to carry on tradition and capture the smoky phenolics (aromas) once native and unavoidable to the malting process and the final spirit product.

MASHING USING MALTED GRAIN

A standard mash is the process of holding your grains at what is known as saccharification, which refers to the process of starch being broken down to its smaller, simpler components. This includes sugars such as glucose, maltose, and maltotriose. These sugars become food for the yeast to eat.

If you're going to make whiskey, or any other spirit from grain, you're going to want to understand the mashing process. The process consists of steeping grain in hot water to activate enzymes and convert starches into sugars. It's an important step in the distilling process for any spirit made from grain. Mashing with malted grains (remember, often referred to just as malt when it's barley) will most likely contain all the enzymes you need to convert your starches into simple sugars.

If you're using raw grains, you'll perform a cereal mash first before performing a traditional mash (see "Cereal Mashing" on page 28). Using a combination of malted grain and raw grain in distilling is quite popular; it is how spirits like bourbon are made. A single malt whiskey uses 100 percent malted barley. For that reason, is a bit easier for a home distiller to mash, and a great place to start your mashing journey.

THE MASHING PROCESS

The basics of mashing are quite simple. A grain bill that uses only two-row barley malt, like those in a Scotch or all-malt whiskey, means that if we crush our grains we have access to the enzymes and starch, all ready for mashing.

You'll use the enzymes in the grain to convert your starch to sugar. These enzymes are activated in water at a temperature of around 130°F (54°C) and deactivated around 170°F (77°C). You'll want to "dough in," which means you'll be adding your grains to water that has been preheated. You'll use 1.25 quarts (1.2 liters) of water per pound (one half kilogram) of grain when you're mashing, though you can vary this depending on the type of grains and your mash tun. Using a large spoon or mash paddle, you should stir the grains as you slowly add them. Any dry spots in your mash means you won't be converting that starch into sugar.

The ideal temperature to hold your mash is around 148°F (64°C), so plan on aiming to hold between 145°F and 150°F (63°C and 66°C), which is where alpha and beta amylase enzymes in the mash are near their peak operating temperature and able to effectively convert the starch to sugar. To hit this temperature your original "strike water," or the water you've added your grains to, needs to be about one degree higher per pound of grain than your target temperature. If you are able to hold in the ideal temperature range the conversion process takes no less than twenty minutes, but often we try to hold these temperatures for sixty minutes to make sure as much starch as possible is converted into sugar. Stirring the mash grains during this time isn't necessary, but you may, especially if you're heating a kettle from the bottom and aren't using a pump to recirculate the hot liquid that's at the bottom of the kettle. When closing your mash up in an insulated cooler, it's best to let it sit. If you're using a pump to recirculate the wort, there's no real need to stir your grains; it's often better to let your mash bed settle and "set" during the process.

CHECKING YOUR CONVERTED MASH

Iodine can be added to a small sample of mash liquid to see if starch conversion has occurred. If the liquid stays dark blue or purple in the sample, you know a large amount of long chain sugars and starches still exist. If the sample turns red, starches are in the process of being broken down, but saccharification hasn't finished. When the iodine turns light orange or yellow, you know that saccharification is complete and your mash is mostly simple sugars ready to be rinsed from the grain to be absorbed by yeast during fermentation!

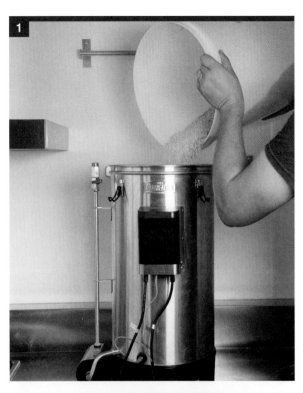

SPARGING YOUR GRAIN AND COOLING YOUR WORT

After you've held your mash for sixty minutes, it's time to rinse the grain, or sparge the grains. This is also called "mashing out." This requires a second kettle or vessel to heat and hold 180°F (82°C) water. Using hot water stops the mashing process and aids in rinsing the grain.

The amount of water to have on hand will be 50 percent more than you mashed with. You may not use all of this. So, if you mashed with 4 gallons (15 liters) of water, you'll want to have 6 gallons (23 liters) of sparge water at the ready. Gently add some of the water to the top of your mash tun if you can, so your grains are completely covered in liquid, trying not to disturb the grain bed. If you are using a mash tun or vessel with a valve, you can start running off your mash into a small container, opening the valve one third of the way.

You'll want to collect these first runnings in small amounts, closing your valve after a quart or so, putting this wash back on top of your grain bed until you see the wash running clear from the bottom valve. If you're not sure what to look for, continue this process for a little while; you'll see large chunks of husk material, as well as cloudy protein-rich wash, slowly turn clear.

Once clear, open your valve one quarter of the way and begin collecting in your kettle first, or directly to your fermentation vessel. Slowly add your sparge water to the top of your mash vessel as your wort runs out, keeping a layer of liquid on top of the grain bed. If you're collecting for a 5-gallon (19-liter) batch, stop adding sparge water after 4.5 gallons (17 liters) are collected in your cleaned and sanitized fermentation vessel. Let the last of your wort in your mash tun empty out into your fermentation vessel until you've collected around 5.25 gallons (20 liters).

To naturally cool your wort, you may have to let it sit for 24 hours. At the very least, you don't want to pitch, or add, your yeast until the temperature is below 90°F (32°C). Anything above this may kill the yeast. Ideally your yeast package will list the optimal temperature range to pitch the yeast to your wort. Alternatively if you're using a kettle, bucket, or fermenter with a large-enough opening, you may want to invest in an immersion chiller, a copper coil that you immerse in your wort and run cold water through to cool much more quickly. You may also have a tub or sink large enough to add cold water and ice or ice packs to and immerse the entire fermenter in the ice water bath. Some electric brewing systems come with a chiller, like the Grainfather, which comes with a counterflow chiller (CFC) and is meant to be hooked up to a pump and a water faucet for chilling and transferring of the wort (pictured on page 17).

(1) Electric brewing systems contain a mash basket for your crushed grain. **(2)** Once you've steeped the crushed grain at sacchrification temperature, it's time remove the basket from the boiler. **(3)** Be sure to have additional water at the ready to rinse your grains. **(4)** Pour the water evenly over your grain bed, trying not to let the water dig in to the grain bed much.

CEREAL MASHING

Although this step would be done before sacchrification, or a standard mashing process, because of its complexity I've left it for last. It's best to understand single-step, single-temperature sacchrification mashing first. But, for many distillers who want to make grain-based spirit from raw, unmalted grains, an understanding of cereal mashing is needed.

Cereal mashing is great. It allows you access to any type of grain for distilling. Raw grain is often cheaper and more accessible than malted grain. Still a pre-ferred method for some distillers, cereal mashing has been employed for a long time in distilling. It can be used to produce bourbon, corn whiskey, and rye whiskey.

The process of cereal mashing is a bit loose and varied, which also allows you to be less precise. So, if you understand the steps it takes, and follow trusted recipes at first, you'll get excellent results from cereal mashing unmalted grain.

Corn typically requires a different mill than malted grains.

GELATINIZATION

Gelatinization is a key component to cereal mashing. Gelatinization is an important first step in cereal mashing to make the starch in raw grain readily available to enzymes. Oftentimes distillers refer to "cooking" their grains, and technically what they're doing is gelatinizing their grains.

If it's possible, first break your grain through grinding or milling. Although difficult with raw grain that is quite hard or fresh grain with high moisture content, breaking your grain will make the process much quicker and easier.

Adding enough water to cover the grain is the next step. The amount of water during gelatinization isn't so important, but it's best to cover your grains. In my home kettle, I put about 1 inch of water above my grains.

As the grains absorb water and swell, you may be left with a sticky mush that's hard to stir if there isn't enough water. It may thicken to the point that it scorches on the heat source. You should always add more water as you go, if needed.

Gelatinization is best done by slowly bringing up the temperature of the grain and water until gelatinization occurs, which is different for every grain. Many people just bring their grains to a boil and then let them cool. I recommend this as it speeds up the gelatinization process. Some grains such as wheat and rye don't actually need the high temperatures to gelatinize.

Your porridge of water and grain should get gooey and thicken as the starch begins to break down. It thickens because the starch has been released into the water. As you stir, the porridge should start to cling to your mixing spoon but slide off, like runny yogurt, often leaving a starchy layer on the spoon. Now that you've achieved getting the starch out of hiding, you're ready for the next cereal mashing step: liquefaction.

LIQUEFACTION

Liquefaction is literally the process of liquefying your starch. Liquefaction begins to break the starch down through alpha-amylase (AA) enzyme activity. Alpha-amylase is an expert cutter of long-chain starch molecules into smaller, more manageable sugars and dextrins.

The alpha-amylase enzyme comes in different formats from different natural sources: plants, bacteria, and fungi. Most are dried and powdered. All work well, but the most sought after are alpha-amylase that can work at high temperatures. These can be added during the gelatinization stage, and bringing your grains to a boil doesn't deactivate these enzymes.

Lower-temperature alpha-amylase enzyme can also be used for saccharification. Notice it likes a lower pH, which can be good if you're trying to break down fruit. Medium-temperature alpha-amylase enzymes are quite common and very general-purpose, often recommended for grains in the lower gelatinization temperature range, as it can liquefy as you gelatinize. High-temperature alpha-amylase is great for those grains that need a bit more heat to gelatinize.

GRAIN	MINIMUM GELATINIZATION TEMPERATURE
Corn	170°F (77°C)
Barley	144°F (62°C)
Wheat	150°F (66°C)
Rye	142°F (61°C)
Oats	146°F (63°C)
Rice	180°F (82°C)
Potato	160°F (71°C)
Sorghum	167°F (75°C)

GENERAL NAME	SOURCE ORGANISM	TEMPERATURE RANGE	FUNCTION
Low-Temperature Alpha-Amylase	Fungal	70–140°F (21–60°C)	Liquefaction/ Saccharification
Medium-Temperature Alpha-Amylase	Bacterial	120–170°F (49–77°C)	Liquefaction
High-Temperature Alpha-Amylase	Bacterial	175–212°F (79–100°C)	Liquefaction
Malted Barley Alpha-Amylase	Plant	148–167°F (64–75°C)	Liquefaction

You'll know when liquefaction has occurred when the stirring gets easier. A well-liquefied cereal mash will be easy to turn into simple sugar. Be patient: This process can take 20 to 30 minutes, or even up to 2 hours, so give it some time.

SACCHARIFICATION

If you read earlier about mashing malted grain, you'll understand that this is the same step. To review, saccharification is a traditional single temperature mashing step used to convert starch to sugars. The goal now is to take your mixture of hydrolyzed starch, now in the form of dextrins, and make it into absorbable yeast food. Remember, without converting dextrins down further to simple sugars, the yeast can't create the ethanol we hope to collect and enjoy at the end of the distilling process.

At this point in cereal mashing, depending on your recipe, malted grain may be added for both its own starch and enzymes, and a standard saccharification mash at between 145°F and 150°F (63°C and 66°C) could be completed. Malted grain high in diastatic power (high in amylase enzymes) is needed to convert all of the long-chain sugars in your cereal mash. This malted

grain may just be called base malt, two-row malt, six-row malt, and, if it's really high in enzymatic activity, distiller's malt. A good rule is to add at least 30 percent or more malted barley to have ample enzyme activity able to convert dextrins to simple sugars.

Not adding more grains? Another way to saccharify your mash is to add exogenous enzyme. There are numerous choices, with some working best at lower temperatures, often around 140°F (60°C) or less.

Glucoamylase (amyloglucosidase) enzyme is the most recommended enzyme for this last step in the cereal mashing process. It's extremely efficient and works in mashes that may be somewhat acidic. Beta-amylase is the common enzyme in barley and can also be found on the shelf in fungal form ready to be added to your mash.

Depending on the number of enzymes, active saccharification can take anywhere between 20 to 90 minutes when using raw grain. As we discussed before, look to hold saccharification temperatures for about 1 hour, after which your starches should be fully converted to sugars. To finish mashing, follow the "Sparging Your Grain and Cooling Your Wort" process that we discussed on page 27.

EXOGENOUS ENZYMES FOR SACCHARIFICATION WHEN CEREAL MASHING			
GENERAL NAME	TYPICAL SOURCE	TEMPERATURE RANGE	OPTIMAL PH RANGE
Glucoamylase	Fungal	65–140°F (18–40°C)	3.0–5.5
Beta-amylase	Fungal	65–140°F (18–40°C)	3.0–5.5
Beta-amylase	Malted Barley	130–150°F (54–66°C)	5.0–5.7

FERMENTING
Chapter 2

Whether this is the beginning of your distilling journey or you've just finished mashing grains (see the previous chapter), fermentation is similar across all spirits you may make. In fact, learning the fermentation process may give you the confidence to branch out into making other alcoholic beverages like wine, beer, and cider. The fermentation processes are the same. It's the distilling stage following fermentation that differentiates spirits from other alcoholic beverages.

A wash is what we're fermenting! Wash is initially sugar, water, and yeast. Once fermented, it's mostly alcohol and water. It might also contain some additional nutrients and enzymes to help the yeast thrive during the fermentation process. Your sugar could come from any source and may even define what sort of spirit you're making. All types of fruit, a mash of grains, corn sugar, molasses, or honey, just to name a few sugar sources, could be used. Yeast needs both water and sugar to create a wash that can be distilled. A wash could be table sugar and water dissolved together with yeast added for fermentation. In the case of table sugar, we would typically also add nutrients, or use turbo yeast that contains nutrients and yeast in one package, which keeps the yeast healthy and active during the fermentation. Let's take a closer look at some of the sugars and ingredients you'll use for your wash.

Some distillers refer to a wash as wort when made from grain. The wort, when fermented, becomes a "beer." The only real differences between this beer and the beer you drink is the beer you drink has hops added and it's carbonated and cooled for serving. Otherwise, the grains and process are pretty much the same! Grapes that are pressed but still unfermented are simply "juice" (think grape juice) that becomes "wine" after it becomes alcoholic and fermentation is finished. The difference here is that the wine is bound for the still, probably to become brandy. Otherwise, after fermentation, it may have been bottled and ready to drink as any other wine. Whether grape or grain, they provide sugars to be fermented into alcohol that might be bound for the still instead of the bottle!

FERMENTATION INGREDIENTS

Let's start with your sugar source. The source of your sugar often determines the type of spirit that you're making; however, most sugar sources are quite versatile when it comes to making spirits. But, in some instances, such as a Scottish-style single malt whiskey, you will always be using barley malt. In the case of American bourbon whiskey, corn as well. Let's start there, with fermenting grain.

GRAIN

Grain is a favorite base for a wash of distillers around the world. Malted grain, or simply just malt when referring to barley, is an excellent base for fermentation. The great thing about grain is that it contains a lot of nutrients for the yeast. Unlike some other sugar washes, a grain wash might be a bit lower in alcohol by volume, typically because a large amount of grain, as well as more equipment, is required to create an alcoholic wash from a grain mash (see Chapter 1). Consider the flip side: using a processed sugar like sucrose (cane sugar), which simply needs to be diluted in water.

Grain can be used to make whiskeys, gins, and vodkas. The easiest to use, malt (barley) is used in most whiskeys. It can also be used to make gin or vodka. Most commercial distilleries target around 8 percent alcohol by volume (ABV) for their wash. Although malt varies, as well as the efficiency (amount of sugar extracted) of a mash, this would be about 15 pounds (7 kilograms) of two-row barley malt for a 5-gallon (19-liter) wash. The target ABV percent of a grain wash for whiskey can be lower or higher but is typically in the 6 to 12 percent range. The ABV percent could be even higher for a vodka, where high alcohol content is helpful in the distillation process. Anything lower than 6 percent ABV in a finished grain wash may not produce much spirit for the same amount of labor that would have gone into a higher ABV wash.

CONSIDER MALT EXTRACT

Malt extract is the mashing process of grain done for you. It is a syrupy, sticky extract of barley in liquid form, often known as liquid malt extract (LME). It can also be dried to a powder known as dried malt extract (DME). It's a great way to begin making whiskeys and other grain-based spirits without the mashing. Because the process of mashing is done for you, and the wash has essentially been evaporated into a syrup, the product is a bit more expensive than doing it yourself. Twelve pounds (5 kilograms) of liquid malt extract, or 9 pounds (4 kilograms) of dried malt extract, will give you a wash near 8 percent ABV. See the recipe in Chapter 10 for a great first whiskey recipe using malt extract.

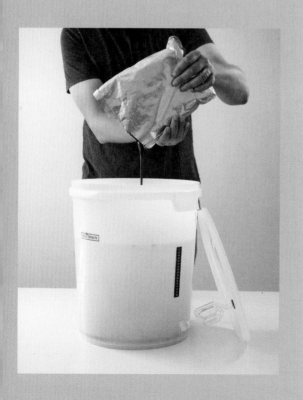

FRUITS AND VEGETABLES

Fruits are a fun fermentation project and make a great wash. Often fruit adds its flavor to the finished spirit, creating a lovely brandy reminiscent of the fruit you harvested, foraged, or purchased. Fruit varies significantly in its sugar content but fructose, the sugar present in fruit, is easily fermentable. For fermentation, fruit is often frozen and then thawed to break down the cellular structure; from fresh or frozen it is then crushed, pressed, squeezed, or mashed directly into the fermenter or other large bucket or collection vessel. The yeast has an easier time getting to the sugar in liquid form than trying to get to it through the solid fruit flesh or skin.

Although fruit is the core of any brandy, it can also be used for schnapps, liqueurs, gins, and vodkas. The most common fruits used for fermentation are apples, pears, and grapes. The easiest way to use fruit in fermentation is to start with pure fruit juice. You can also use fruit concentrate, which can help increase the level of alcohol in your fermentation quite quickly as it's not as diluted as juice. Sometimes fruit and sugar are added to the same wash to increase the ABV potential of the fermentation. Some fruits may give you only 4 to 5 percent ABV in a wash, quite low compared to most washes. Grapes, on the other hand, are little sugar vessels and, just as in wine, may give you sugar that produces a wash (or wine) from 12 to 14 percent. Just remember: the more you can break down the fruit, the better chance it has to completely ferment. Fresh fruit is often added to a fermenter in a nylon bag or in a muslin cloth so that the leftover solid matter can be removed at the end of fermentation. Prior to that, leave it in—it still contains some sugar!

Vegetables are a different beast from fruit altogether. Although vegetables like potatoes can be a cheap option for starches (complex sugars that need to be mashed), they can be quite hard to work with. A typical vegetable mash is done in a kettle until the vegetable is completely mushy and broken down, and either grain or enzyme is added. We'll talk more about vegetable wash fermentation and mashing later when we discuss vodka recipes, but also review Chapter 1 on mashing to start understanding the process and the goals.

Fruit can provide sugar for your fermentation, especially if you're looking to make brandy.

SUGARS

Although all washes are made of sugar, when we typically use the phrase "sugar wash" we mean the use of a basic or processed sugar of some sort, most often corn sugar (dextrose) or table sugar (sucrose.) Sugars occur naturally in plants like sugar cane and sugar beets, and is how refined crystallized sugars like sucrose are made.

Some examples of other naturally occurring sugars (outside of fruits and vegetables) would be sugar cane juice, agave syrup, molasses, and honey. Typically sugars like corn sugar and table sugar are used to make gin or vodka. In some cases, they might also make moonshine, schnapps, or other liqueurs. Natural and refined sugars are very good at making clear spirits that have a neutral flavor.

Molasses, a by-product of the sugar refining process but essentially a sugary substance, is the main ingredient in rum and contains other things besides sugar such as minerals and nutrients that account for the dark color. Sugar cane juice that is not processed is also used in distilling, especially in Brazil to make cachaça. Agave is the main ingredient in mezcals, such as tequila.

Sugar washes can be quite high in alcohol, sometimes upward of 18 percent ABV. Although you can use pure sugar to make a high ABV wash, it helps to include nutrients (processed sugar contains no nutrients) for a successful sugar fermentation. It takes about 20 pounds (9 kilograms) of corn sugar to make a 16 percent ABV wash. Standard white table sugar, or sucrose, is more efficient: It only takes about 16 pounds (7 kilograms) to make a 16 percent ABV wash. All that's missing from a successful fermentation is some yeast and nutrients.

WHAT EXACTLY IS MOONSHINE?

Moonshine is typically a whiskey made from straight corn or corn sugar, although it can be made from table sugar, malted barley, or any number of grains or sugars. It's best to think of it as an unaged whiskey. Throw a little oak in there and you might have something more akin to bourbon!

YEAST

Yeast is a single-celled fungus that absorbs sugars during fermentation and creates alcohols and carbon dioxide (CO_2) as a by-product. Yeast replicates and dies during the fermentation process, creating lees (also called trub, mostly during whiskey fermentations), a collection of dead yeast at the bottom of the fermenter. This process continues until there are no simple sugars left in the fermenter for the yeast to absorb. It might also end if they run out of nutrients or if the fermentation environment changes and becomes too hot or cold.

One of the most critical components to a successful fermentation and for flavor development in aged products like rums and whiskeys is the strain of yeast you choose. Yeast you can purchase that work well for distilling include turbo, ale, wine, or spirit-specific yeast. Most high-quality yeast will ferment quickly and efficiently. One thing to keep in mind when selecting a yeast strain is that there is probably a specific yeast out there for the spirit you would like to make and finding this strain of yeast will help guarantee a successful fermentation. Some yeasts are better with certain sugars, better at higher alcohol fermentations, and better at creating specific flavors you'd want in your spirit.

IS TURBO YEAST ANY GOOD?

There's a myth that turbo yeast was developed for the fuel industry—that just isn't true. Because of the illegality of distilling in most countries, turbo yeast was developed for fast and effective fermentations, not a bad thing for us distillers. Turbo yeast simply contains a yeast with a high alcohol tolerance and a large amount of yeast nutrient included. Sometimes enzymes are also included to help break down more complex sugars in the fermenter as well. Turbo yeast is ideal for sugar washes of corn sugar (dextrose) or table sugar (sucrose) when you'd like to obtain a neutral spirit for flavoring, or for gin or vodka. However, it can be successfully used for practically any other spirit as well.

There's yeast specific to distilling, though you can use just about any good home brewing yeast. A beer, wine, or distiller's yeast will provide more consistent results than those you find for bread as the strain has been cultured for liquid fermentation and the creation of alcohol.

You will pick up on the fact that many distillers use bread yeast from their local grocery store. This is okay, but you just need to be aware that bread yeast is not sold or grown in laboratories for the production of alcohol or for its flavor attributes in a wash. They will still produce alcohol; however, the results might be quite variable in terms of fermentation and flavor. Another common grocery store item is tomato paste, to make the now "internet famous" tomato paste wash (TPW). I won't go into detail here, but tomato paste seems to act as a nutrient for yeast, although the nutritional label seems to suggest otherwise. Many folks have created successful washes that have contained tomato paste but have also contained other ingredients that might be as, or more, helpful. Whether tomato paste itself is particularly useful, I'm not sure, but if you'd like to give it a try there's plenty of info out there.

One of the most important things to understand about your yeast is its alcohol tolerance. If you plan to make a sugar wash up to 16 percent ABV and your yeast can only manage to ferment to 10 percent ABV, you'll leave sugar behind in your fermenter that won't be turned into alcohol to be distilled out in your still.

To get started, you can select a yeast for whiskey by finding a specific whiskey yeast, or an ale yeast or a beer yeast, that has an alcohol tolerance somewhere around 8 to 10 percent ABV or higher. If you're looking to make a brandy, you might not find a brandy yeast, but you will quite quickly find a wine yeast happy to ferment your fruit. Most people choose to use a yeast with high alcohol potential and also add a large amount of nutrient when fermenting sucrose and dextrose sugar (most likely be a turbo yeast, which is already a combination of potent yeast and nutrient). If you are unsure of the amount to use, a typical sachet of pure yeast from a home brew store can ferment 5 gallons (19 liters). To be on the safe side, pitching (adding) 1 gram of dry yeast per liter, or about 4 grams per gallon, is a good rule of thumb. Turbo yeast is mostly nutrient, not yeast, so it's best to follow the instructions. Yeast also comes in liquid form for brewing and distilling (again, best to follow the instructions). Pitching the entire sachet or container into 3 to 5 gallons (12 to 19 liters) should be enough, as it's designed for this batch size.

Fermentation temperatures are dictated by the type of yeast and should be included on the pack of yeast you purchased. Room temperature 70°F (21°C) is typically fine for wash fermentations. Fermenting on the hotter end of the yeast's range can create more flavor development through ester creation (good for dark, aged spirits) and can also lead to a faster fermentation. An average range for many distilling yeasts is 64°F to 86°F (18°C to 30°C), though some yeasts can ferment even hotter! Yeasts that like it cooler than 64°F (18°C) are typically lager yeasts for beer brewing and are not often used for spirits.

YEAST NUTRIENTS AND ENZYMES

There are many general yeast nutrients out there that contain a well-balanced nutritional plan for yeast during fermentation. These can be added as per instructions. They often include things like diammonium phosphate, a source of free amino nitrogen (FAN) critical to yeast health that yeast won't get from things like sucrose, dextrose, or even some fruits. Other vitamins and minerals will allow them to build strong cell walls, as well as increase the yeast's metabolism and increase its ability to replicate, making it overall healthier and more effective. If you are fermenting a sugar wash, don't forget the nutrients! Brands of yeast blends you might find are Fermax, Fermaid, and Yeastex, though many yeast companies, such as White Labs and Wyeast, supply nutrients as well.

As in mashing, enzymes are sometimes added to fermentation to be sure complex carbohydrates are completely processed down to simple sugars for the yeast. Enzymes naturally regulate and accelerate chemical reactions. Alpha-amylase and glucoamylase enzymes that aid in the breaking down of starches in grain during mashing can do the same for complex sugars during fermentation and can be quite beneficial on fruit carbohydrates (starches and sugars) during fermentation as well. Apple varieties can be starchy and are a good example of a fruit that can benefit from fermentation enzymes.

These nutrients and enzymes are less critical in whiskeys in which you've mashed grain. Malted barley and other grains contain plenty of nutrients and enzymes. Unless you've added more simple sugars to your wash postmash, a fermented grain mash should have ample nutrients and minerals for the yeast, though adding more per your yeast nutrient's recommendation won't hurt!

Measuring nutrients on a scale will give you accuracy and repeatability.

CLEANING, SANITIZING, AND OTHER CONSUMABLES

It's worth talking about cleaners (or cleansers) and sanitizers. One of the tasks home distillers love or loathe (mostly loathe, I think) is cleaning and sanitizing. It can take up the majority of any day focused on the hobby, no matter what step of the process you're in. Especially with fermentation equipment, it's probably one of the most critical steps in the process. Having clean and sanitized fermentation equipment almost guarantees you great results.

Cleaning is the process we use to remove noticeable and visible residue, dirt, muck, and junk from our gear. It is the first step in the process toward clean equipment. Cleaning can be done with household items such as dish soap; however, dish soap is often scented and may leave a residue that affects your product's flavor—not good. Percarbonate cleaners have become quite popular in home distilling. They contain sodium carbonate and hydrogen peroxide. A popular brand of percarbonate cleaner is Five Star Chemicals's Powdered Brewery Wash (PBW). If used properly, this can clean the grime off of most surfaces.

Sanitizing is the second step, typically done the day of fermentation just prior to the use of your already clean equipment. When you're sanitizing, you're making sure your equipment is free of bacteria and wild yeasts that may affect your fermentation. Acid sanitizers are popular, and Five Star Chemicals also have one of the best-known sanitizers for home distilling, Star San. Star San is a no-rinse sanitizer, meaning it's safe to consume, and it can sit in most fermenters until you're ready to add your wash. Iodine sanitizers such as Iodophor are also still used, but less frequently, these days.

A few other things you may encounter on your fermentation journey:

Fermentation Carbon: Sometimes carbon is added to remove impurities created during fermentation. The most popular is Still Spirits Turbo Carbon. This is the same as the activated carbon you may use later during the polishing process, often packaged a bit differently.

Fermentation Clarifier: Typically a two-part clarifier that contains chitosan and kieselsol, this helps clarify your wash prior to adding it to your still. Great if you have a very hazy wash filled with yeast and protein, the clarifier will help both settle to the bottom of your fermenter. Still Spirits Turbo Clear, and Liquor Quik Super-Kleer K.C., and other options are available.

pH Testing: pH can affect your fermentation, so being able to take a reading when things don't seem to be going right can be helpful. Fermentation pH levels should be between 3.4 and 5.5, with a target between 4.0 and 4.5.

FERMENTING EQUIPMENT

If you don't currently have a fermenter already, one of the first (or second, if you don't have a still yet) things you'll do is choose an appropriate fermenter. The size should be slightly larger than the batch size you plan on distilling, as you'll need some headroom for the fermentation activity. The fermenter size may be much larger than your still if you're producing fermented wash for multiple runs on your still. Smaller fermenters than your still don't make much sense because you'll have to run multiple fermentations, and possibly own multiple fermenters, to fill your still.

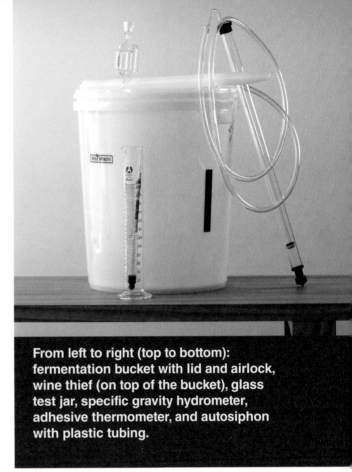

From left to right (top to bottom): fermentation bucket with lid and airlock, wine thief (on top of the bucket), glass test jar, specific gravity hydrometer, adhesive thermometer, and autosiphon with plastic tubing.

Small fermenters can be fun to keep around for experimentation, but distilling is already a process during which we're leaving a good amount of the wash behind in the boiler, so a small fermentation often means a much smaller amount of spirit collected. Though most stills can run small batches if you'd like, most times a wash can sit in the fermenter for a few weeks before it is used. Once your wash is fermented, it has a hard time growing much bacteria or getting infected because it has a bunch of alcohol in it. It's okay to not use it all right away.

So what are your options for fermenters? The most common is a 6.5-gallon (25-liter) bucket. These typically come with an airtight lid and a rubber grommet in the top of the lid that can take an airlock. A bucket specifically designed for fermentation will also have graduation marks so you know how big of a batch you are making. This is a great way to start fermenting.

Another option is a glass carboy, now considered an old-school method of fermenting that is still preferred by many distillers. Glass is easy to clean, and you can see inside of it, which allows you to watch the excitement that goes on during fermentation. Glass carboys have started to be replaced by polyethylene terephthalate (PET) carboys lately. PET is a tough and durable plastic that works very well as a fermenter. Other fermenters may be plastic barrel-shaped containers, small glass jugs, or large glass demijohns. Some might even just be a large plastic food-grade garbage can—if it can be cleaned and sanitized and sealed well, it doesn't need to be fancy.

Another common but significantly more expensive fermenter is a stainless-steel conical fermenter. These look cool but can be overkill for what you're trying to do as a home distiller, though they are easy to clean and will last a long time. Stainless steel may be the choice of many professionals, but it isn't a requirement for a good fermentation or to make high-quality spirits. If you happen to have a stainless fermenter, that's great! If you're just starting off in distillation, it can be more than you need, but don't let me discourage you from getting one (I might just have three).

Besides the fermenter itself, you will need a few other fermenting accessories. Most critical is an airlock, as well as a rubber stopper or rubber grommet for the airlock to fit into at the top of your fermenter. Airlocks come in numerous shapes and sizes. All of them require that you fill them with clean water or vodka. Many people like to use vodka as it won't contaminate your fermentation should it accidentally get sucked in. Common airlocks are three-piece airlocks, S-locks (sometimes referred to as "double bubble" airlocks), and two-piece airlocks. In some cases, you may just want to run plastic tubing to a jar of water (just be sure the tubing is well secured, and air can't get into your fermentation), which also creates an airlock: CO_2 can escape during fermentation but air cannot get into your fermentation (the true purpose of any good airlock).

Another useful item to have around is a specific gravity hydrometer, also known as a triple scale hydrometer. This is used to determine the amount of sugar in your wash when you start fermenting, and the amount of sugar left after the majority, if not all, has been used by the yeast. Specific gravity (SG) is based on water, which is measured at an SG of 1.000. Original gravity (OG) is the specific gravity your wash starts at, the original reading you take before fermenting. Your reading will be greater than 1.000 because sugars are denser than water. Final gravity (FG) is the specific gravity your wash ends at, which will be a number lower than your OG as the yeast uses the sugar and creates alcohol. Alcohol is lighter than water, which has an SG of 1.000, so your FG may read as low as .990.

A hydrometer floats, and you may use it directly in your fermenter or you may take a sample of wash out of the fermenter with a wine thief or a cleaned and sanitized pitcher or small flask. Your fermenter may also have a valve on it for taking samples. A plastic or glass test jar (or "test cylinder," as it may be called) between 250 and 500 milliliters is a good place to test your wash. You will be able to float your hydrometer in the test jar and take a very accurate reading at the surface of the liquid while it is floating.

An adhesive thermometer for the side of your fermenter will let you know if your wash is still in your yeast's preferred fermentation temperature range. You can also buy a glass floating thermometer or metal dial thermometer often used in cooking to measure the temperature of your wash. This also comes in handy when taking gravity readings using your hydrometer.

A racking cane with plastic tubing or an autosiphon will be helpful to move your wash into your still, leaving the yeast and sediment on the bottom behind. A faster but less controlled method of transfer is to simply dump your wash from the fermenter into the still, but you may transfer a large amount of yeast and sediment from the bottom of the fermenter, which can scorch in your still's boiler. A nylon or muslin cloth set in a large funnel may help capture some of this while you pour into your boiler.

If you're adding sugar to water, a long stainless or plastic spoon or paddle will come in handy. Be sure it can reach the bottom of your fermenter or you may not dissolve all of your sugar into solutions well enough for the yeast to eat it. This spoon or paddle may also be used to mash fruit in your fermenter should you make a fruit wash from soft fruit such as blueberries, strawberries, or peaches.

Let's see how to put all of this equipment to use.

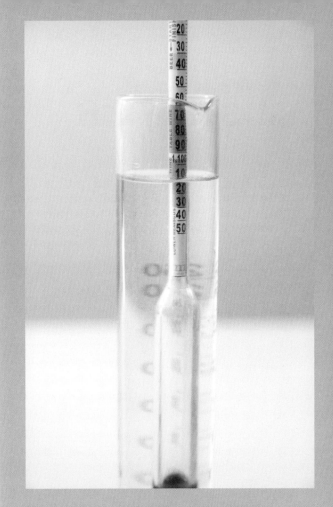

WHAT IS SPECIFIC GRAVITY?

Specific gravity (SG) is a measure of the density of your wash. Water is 1.000 and a reading lighter than that is a substance lighter than water. Sugar adds density to water. As the sugar is eaten, alcohol (mostly ethanol) is created, which is lighter than water. Often a complete fermentation of a sugar wash will finish with a specific gravity of .990, as the alcohol makes the overall makeup of the wash lighter than water.

MAKING A
SUGAR WASH

The easiest way to start fermenting (and really, distilling) is to make a sugar wash. A good, healthy, happy sugar wash can be done in about ten days. From this standard sugar wash, you can make neutral spirit, moonshine, schnapps, vodka, gin, or flavor with essences.

▸ Makes around 5 gallons (19 liters) of wash

▸ Original Gravity (OG): 1.1109–1.1113 | Final Gravity (FG): 0.990–0.998 | Alcohol by Volume (ABV): 14–15%

MAKE THE WASH

1. Clean and sanitize all equipment you'll be using for fermentation and set on a clean and sanitized surface.

2. Add the 150 g of Distiller's Nutrient Light Spirits to your clean and sanitized fermenter.

3. Fill the fermentation vessel with 3 gallons (11 liters) of water at around 92°F (33°C), and slowly pour and stir in the 15 lb. of dextrose a few pounds at a time.

YOU WILL NEED:

▸ **6-gallon (23-liter) or larger fermenter**

▸ **Lid and airlock for fermenter**

▸ **250 ml glass or plastic test jar**

▸ **Wine thief (optional)**

▸ **5 oz (150 g) Still Spirits Distiller's Nutrient Light Spirits**

▸ **15 lb. (7 kg) dextrose (corn sugar)**

▸ **20 g Still Spirits Distiller's Yeast (vodka or gin)**

(2) Fill the fermenter with water. (3) Add your sugar. (4) Stir until the sugar is completely dissolved. (5) Add the yeast direct from 20 g sachet or measured out.

4. Stir vigorously until it's completely dissolved.

5. Once the sugar is fully stirred in and dissolved, top up the fermenter with another 2 gallons (8 liters) of room temperature water, and stir for a few seconds.

6. Take a specific gravity reading by pulling out a sample of the wash with your wine thief (or by simply dipping your test jar in the top of the wash).

7. Float the hydrometer in the test jar and look at the line at the top of the wash. It should read about 1.111 (or between 1.108 and 1.114). Read your hydrometer's instructions for temperature correction.

8. Add the distiller's yeast directly to the liquid, sprinkling over the top. The yeast will dissolve into the solution with time.

9. Close your fermenter with a lid or stopper, as well as an airlock, and leave to ferment at around 72°F (22°C), being sure to keep it between 67 and 75°F (19 and 24°C) for at least 14 days.

10. Watch for bubbling in your airlock 24 to 48 hours later to make sure fermentation has started. If not, you may need to adjust your temperature or repitch your yeast.

11. Once bubbling has stopped, you may open your fermenter (or draw off from a spigot) and take a sample of your wash to measure the gravity to be sure it's finished fermenting. If it is below 1.000, probably between 0.990 and 0.994, it is most likely complete and ready to be distilled. If not, raise the fermentation temperature a few degrees and leave it to ferment for another 3 days and check again. Optional: If there seems to be a lot of yeast or protein (big particles floating around) in the wash, you may want a clarifier like Still Spirits Turbo Clear to clarify your wash prior to distilling. Some haziness is okay; we just want to minimize chunks of material in the still.

From here, we'll be transferring the wash into the still. I'm hoping it's the part you've been waiting for, as it's what makes spirits and distilling unique to other homebrewed hobbies. Let's see what we can do with that still!

DISTILLING
Chapter 3

At times it seems that distilling is shrouded in mystery. Liquid goes into a device and comes out different. There is the legacy of information passed on from person to person—trade secrets seem common. Yet the reality is that distilling is and should be no more mysterious than home brewing. I hope by sharing straightforward and easy-to-follow information, this part of the process ultimately becomes one of the least complicated steps in your journey.

That said, there is an art that goes along with the science of distilling. The art of distilling may be one of the harder subjects to take you through, as the artistic process can be quite personal, resulting in amazingly unique spirits. The science is fairly cut and dried. The artistic license you take is why so many spirits are made with similar ingredients and a similar process and yet taste different.

As a distiller, and later on as a blender of cuts or aged spirits, you'll need to take some artistic license without fear: a journey of sensory and flavor discovery, as well as self-discovery. There will be trial and error. You'll make some of the same mistakes every master distiller and blender in a commercial distillery has made and learned from. Relax in that there's very little you can do to completely ruin a spirit. The still is an excellent tool for purifying a wash, more or less, giving you a distillate that you can treat as a canvas to play with, or to enjoy just as it came out.

Keep in mind that distilling is often mysterious and misunderstood not because it's challenging, but because of the marketing and tall tales you're used to seeing and hearing. Distilleries love selling you an elaborate story. Home distilling existed long before commercial distilling, and both processes mirror each other in many ways. Let's pull the curtain back on what distillers are doing and jump in!

WHAT IS DISTILLING?

Distillation is defined as the separation of alcohol and other substances through evaporation and then condensation of a vapor using a still. Each still is different, and the imperfections in the separation of alcohol, water, and other flavors (congeners, fusels, or fusel alcohols) help determine the final flavor of the spirit.

In this book, and in general, you will see two types of stills: column stills and pot stills. A major difference between stills is the amount of reflux. Reflux happens in each and every still when evaporated liquid falls back down into the still instead of making it to the condenser. If the still refluxes a lot, it is likely happening in a tall column designed to achieve more reflux, often containing plates or packing. The success in separating water and congeners from pure ethanol is greater in these column stills, where the alcohol and water constantly come into contact with physical surfaces and drip back into the boiler, resulting in a cleaner, more neutral ethanol. The path is harder, so lighter vapors like ethanol are separated from water, which is heavier.

In a pot still (also called an alembic still), this reflux happens less, and so the alcohol coming out is essentially dirtier—the light and heavy alcohols blend together, giving the spirit more flavor. It's near impossible to achieve a high ABV (90 to 95 percent) neutral spirit with a pot still, but that often isn't the point. The point of a pot still is finding a balance between alcohol and capturing flavor, making it excellent for aged spirits but less efficient for pure ethanol, which you'd want for a more neutral spirit.

Thus, still design can be valuable to the flavor (or lack thereof) as well as the efficiency a distiller is trying to get. At the same time, many stills are quite versatile and, with a few small adjustments, can change how much reflux they offer and be used for a variety of spirits.

Pulling samples with a copper cylinder to check the gravity midrun.

THE SCIENCE

Distilling doesn't happen without a bit of science, and it'd be a shame if we didn't touch on it. Do you need to understand it all to distill? Nope. In fact, if you have little to no interest in the science behind distillation this section may feel a bit tedious. But read through it and take in what you can: Understanding some of the science behind distillation may help you decide what still is right for you, as well as take you further on in your distilling studies to tweak and modify your process, recipes, and equipment along the way.

Okay, here we go! Everything around us is a collection of atoms and molecules held together by mutual attraction. The temperature of a substance is a measure of the kinetic energy these molecules have. This means the faster the molecules move, the higher the temperature they create. Depending on the substance, and the temperature and pressure applied, the molecules may pack together—like when cold temperatures turn water into ice. But, when heat is applied, molecules speed up and move apart—like when gas escapes from a liquid. This is what your wash does in your still, through evaporation.

Molecules transition from your liquid wash to a gas by having enough heat (that is, energy) to get through a barrier at the surface of the wash. This barrier is created by the fact that the attractive force between molecules is directed inward at the surface of their current substance. Inside the substance, the attractive forces are moving in all directions and cancel each other out. Called surface tension, this force at the surface is stronger and noticeable in liquids like your wash.

The cohesive force between the molecules is stronger between the liquid molecules than with the air molecules: It's what makes them a liquid. They're closer together, so they end up adhering to each other. Because of this, a good amount of energy (that is, heat) is needed to turn your liquid into a gas. We need to overcome the attraction between the molecules in your dense liquid wash. Keep in mind, boiling takes a significant amount of energy. Think about molecules breaking apart from your wash into vapor . . . it's pretty amazing. On top of that, your wash is fighting against becoming vapor through surface tension.

The boiling point for water is 212°F (100°C) at sea level. It has a surface tension of 72.8 millinewtons (mN). (A newton is a measure of force.) Ethanol boils at a lower temperature of 173°F (78°C). It has a surface tension of 22.1 mN. Ethanol's lower surface tension means it has a higher vapor pressure, which means the force it has to remain a liquid between its molecules is weaker than that of water. So, if we left ethanol and water out in a bowl in the sun, the ethanol would evaporate first, as it takes less energy to evaporate.

UNDER PRESSURE

However, we aren't waiting on the sun to do our work! We need to apply enough energy to break the surface tension of our wash effectively and efficiently. When molecules do manage to leave the liquid, their rapid free motion adds to the pressure in an enclosed environment like your still's boiler walls. The vapor pressure created is a measure of the amount of pressure escaped molecules can exert on the surrounding environment and can be measured in your boiler in pounds per square inch (PSI). Some stills may have a pressure rating and come with a dial for you to watch as the pressure builds through the process.

Many stills can safely operate to 20 or 30 PSI, whereas other simple homemade stills that are sealed with tape or flour paste may hold under 1 PSI. They might even leak, which isn't great, as that's good ethanol escaping into the atmosphere! In any case, all stills need to manage a small amount of pressure but may begin to fail quite quickly if the still condenser or outlet gets plugged. If they don't have a pressure-release valve that begins to release pressure on the body, the steam may escape from the next weakest and easiest point out—whether that's where there is flour paste, rivets, lid, or components attached through tri-clamps or other fittings. If that pressure is not allowed to release, it can become explosive (see sidebar).

Fortunately, a still is designed to naturally release excess pressure through the condenser and into your collection vessel. Vapor pressure continues to increase with applied heat (energy). For this reason, you need to make sure you don't release too much vapor pressure at once or the other parts of the still like the condenser won't keep up and your still will look more like a tea kettle blowing off steam—sending precious spirit into the atmosphere as a gas rather than into your collection jars as a liquid. Even worse (and a larger concern than explosions) is a surge of extremely hot liquid coming out of the condenser from your still or from a weak point elsewhere (should pressure build or should too much heat be applied to the boiler). Always keep in mind that you are working with high temperatures and hot liquids!

WHAT ARE THE ODDS OF MY STILL EXPLODING?

If you understand how to use a still and have a commercially or professionally made still, the likelihood of it leaking is far greater than it exploding. In fact, small home stills often can't handle the type of pressure needed to create a massive explosion. Open flames, poor still management, and poor still design are what most often lead to explosions, but even these are few and far between. Could the legends of exploding stills be propaganda to keep people from distilling? I'm not sure, but it seems embedded in our minds that it's something to worry about, when in reality I have never known a distiller with an exploding still.

A pressure gauge is nice to have but is not a requirement.

While the ethanol we're creating through distilling has a high vapor pressure, as the still is run and more and more heat is applied, heavier alcohols and congeners start coming out of the condenser. But first are the lightest molecules; those that have the lowest boiling point like methanol make their way out. These are known as your heads. Distinctly, ethanol makes up the middle portion of the run called the hearts. This is the part of the run we hope to separate off, as the hearts contain the purest form of clean and neutral-flavored alcohol. As the ethanol runs out, it is joined by more solvent-like alcohols, as well as water molecules, often all fused together in a bit of a mish mash with other highly flavorful and aromatic molecules. These "dirty," or maybe a better word is "potent," molecules mix with your alcohol and water, which combine to become known as the final stage of your distillation, your tails. In some cases, these can be saved, often mixed with your hearts to be run through the still again to capture the ethanol it still contains (with less of the other stuff mixed in). On the home scale, if you're making vodka, or a neutral or delicate spirit, you may find it's not worth your while saving a trivial amount of dirty alcohol at the start and finish of your distilling and instead discard it completely.

In a confined space like a still, there is a maximum concentration of molecules from a wash that may be present as vapor at one time. When this point is reached, some vapor needs to transition. Aided by vapor pressure pushing toward a cooler temperature farther away from the heat source, the vapor will eventually come in contact with the water or air-cooled condenser portion of the still near the top, and the vapor becomes saturated again. As this vapor saturates, the molecules condense from vapor back to liquid for collection from the still's condenser. If they didn't make it that far before landing as droplets inside the still somewhere, most likely they'll collect with other droplets and drop back into the boiler as reflux.

Too much vapor and the still will begin to heat up your condenser (cooling arm) faster than it can cool the vapor. A mixture of spirit in liquid form and precious, near-impossible-to-collect alcohol vapor will begin to escape! Controlling the condensation portion of distilling is critical and may require more or less cooling energy (often more or less cooling water) as the distillation process goes on. But it starts by applying the right amount of heat to the boiler so that the vapor pressure doesn't get too high that the condenser can't keep up. Let the process take its course gradually, and it will allow you all of your different boiling points with some amount of segregation.

If we kept the still running, soon all that would be left is a mix of water and heavy congeners, some solid material, and a tiny bit of alcohol in the boiler. We typically don't run our stills dry—the energy it takes at the end to collect any alcohol is limited, and often that alcohol isn't great. We instead focus on the middle of the run, the good stuff, the hearts, the ethanol, collecting it in cuts, fractions as we go, with small additions of heads and tails to add aroma and flavor.

Dissecting a still run into cuts and then blending the components is both an art and science, but selecting that heart of ethanol and separating it out is our primary goal, even as we blend back in nonethanol stuff from the first heads and the last tails of our run later.

EXTRACTION

Ethanol is the most critical for us to extract. It's the alcohol we enjoy drinking, the stuff our body doesn't reject. However, there are other alcohols present in most washes and distilling runs. By managing your still temperatures, you might find each of these alcohols and compounds (as a collective congeners or esters) easily identified by their different tastes and smells.

BOILING POINTS OF ALCOHOLS AND OTHER MAJOR CHEMICALS		
CHEMICAL	BOILING TEMPERATURE	DESCRIPTION
Acetone	132°F (56°C)	A ketone, smells like nail-polish remover, paint thinner
Methanol	149°F (65°C)	A potentially poisonous alcohol that smells sweet
Ethyl acetate	170°F (77°C)	An ester, fruity sweet odor like pineapple or pear
Ethanol	173°F (78°C)	Neutral alcohol
Isopropyl	180°F (82°C)	Commonly known as rubbing alcohol, bitter flavor
Propyl	207°F (97°C)	Solvent-like alcohol aroma
Butanol	241°F (116°C)	Banana-like flavors and aromas
Amyl alcohols	280°F (138°C)	Fruity, mango, pineapple, and orange like
Furfural	324°F (162°C)	A congener with caramel aroma and flavor

CAN I GO BLIND?

Methanol is deadly stuff, but in the quantities we're dealing with, it is hardly a concern. The amount of methanol varies by the type of sugar source you use. Refined sugars like dextrose and sucrose contain very little methanol. Fruits like grapes and apples contain more methanol. You'll also find some in barley and wheat. You'll ingest methanol eating an apple or drinking orange juice. Of course, it'd take more apples and oranges than you could eat in one sitting to go blind or die! Where methanol becomes deadly is when it is concentrated, if your foreshots are saved, stored, and consumed instead of thrown away. Methanol poisoning can happen with as little as 2 ounces (60 milliliters) of distilled liquid depending on your health and condition. Consuming 8 ounces (237 milliliters) will leave lasting damage, including potential blindness.

So how much are we condensing and collecting? Often much less than what is needed to do harm. While people do still die from moonshine with too much methanol, usually it's because methanol was purchased and added to make the moonshine a greater proof as cheaply as possible.

A good rule of thumb is to immediately discard your foreshots, which is the first 2 ounces (50 milliliters) of distilled liquid for any wash between 1 gallon (4 liters) and 5 gallons (19 liters). They're not worth saving, as even if there's little methanol, they aren't going to taste great. Immediately throw them away, because the last thing you want is an unmarked jar that may have high methanol content. If you aren't careful, you may accidentally end up drinking it or blending it.

Certain bonds form in your wash during fermentation and during the boiling phase that will carry some of these alcohols and organic compounds through with other substances, compounds, and alcohols present. Some show up early, late, or together with ethanol.

Methanol (methyl alcohol) is a poisonous alcohol with an even lower boiling point than ethanol. Methanol is why you need to take foreshots (a small fraction or cut of the first liquid out) at the start of distillation. As the boiler temperature rises, we know where the methanol begins coming out, around 149°F (65°C). Because it may bond with other alcohols like ethanol, you might see small amounts come through for a while as the temperature rises. Yet since we're able to make cuts (fractional, specific amounts throughout the process) during distillation, we can manage to remove more than enough to stay safe. Different cuts will have varying amount of alcohol, purity, flavor, and aroma. Yet we know methanol comes early, and there are heavier congeners with lots of flavor and aroma (sometimes desirable, sometimes not) that will come out last.

To summarize the distillation process:

1. Liquid (wash) becomes vapor in the boiler,

2. Most vapor becomes liquid again inside the still by condensing on the sides or in the column and falling down into the boiler,

3. Further molecular division happens in the boiler as heat rises and various boiling points of the wash are reached,

4. Soon allowing methanol to begin to separate out and escape the wash at the start or the run,

5. Followed by ethanol in the middle, or the heart of the run,

6. And finally a mix of alcohols and congeners, as well as water, to finish off our run.

FREEZE DISTILLATION

Freeze distillation, also known as fractional distillation, takes advantage of the different freezing points of water and alcohol. Since water freezes before alcohol, water can be removed from alcohol in the form of ice. As you remove the water as ice, the alcohol left behind is now more concentrated. This technique is common with home distillers in colder climates and also with beer brewers looking to make traditional beer styles such as eisbock (or other high-alcohol experimental beers). A plastic bottle or jug filled with wash and some patience is all you need. Once the bottle is mostly frozen (60–80% of the way) just tip it out into a collection jar and repeat or enjoy. Note that with this technique, methanol, an unsafe alcohol, is also concentrated. It's always good to proceed with some caution.

There is no perfect way to isolate all methanol in a traditional still. This is because methanol, like all molecules in the boiler, adhere to one another, making them heavier. Water molecules are present, and they weigh on other molecules in the mixture, as water is heavier than methanol. Without the additional reflux a column still offers to break some of these bonds, these molecules continue through the still together, and some of that methanol mixed with other molecules becomes heavier and comes out of the still later on, usually in very small amounts.

DISTILLING EQUIPMENT

The still is the main piece of equipment you'll need on distillation day, so I hope you've decided on one (see Chapter 10 for more on stills)! If you don't have a built-in heat source for your still, this will be your next consideration. A hot plate may work for small stills, but any still running a wash of 5 gallons (19 liters) or more should use a stronger heat source, such as a gas/propane burner or very powerful electric element.

If you are using an electric still, you may want to consider a voltage controller. It typically goes inline between your still and the wall socket. The goal here is to keep the voltage low enough that your still runs at a trickle and doesn't heat up too fast.

If your condenser is cooled by water, you'll need hoses and connections to a faucet. If you don't have this option, you'll want to invest in a submersible pump that can sit in a large container of cool water, like a garbage can. Water needs to be able to recirculate through the condenser to cool the vapor before it escapes.

OTHER IMPORTANT EQUIPMENT

A **proof and tralle hydrometer,** which measures how much alcohol by volume (ABV) is coming from your still, is essential. (It may also be called an alcohol meter or alcometer and only measures ABV.) It's a good idea to take constant measurements throughout the run. It will look similar to a beer/wine hydrometer, but it works differently. The scale is from 0 to 100 percent ABV and may also include 0 to 200 proof. A proof and tralle hydrometer is accurate if the spirit is 68°F (20°C). If the temperature is different you'll need to calibrate your reading to the chart in Appendix B.

> *Note:* ABV, or alcohol by volume, and proof are both measures of alcohol. They are related and can be easily determined if given the other. The percentage of ABV is exactly half of the proof. Or you can look at it as proof being double the ABV percentage. Either way, a 40 percent ABV whiskey will be 80 proof.

You'll want a **set of fifteen to twenty collection jars.** These are what you will fill to make cuts. A 250-milliliter test jar is a great way to make precise cuts and can be a good way to collect from the condenser of your still. You might also want one large jug or bottle to blend back into or various sized containers for blending and consolidating.

A **distiller's parrot** is an excellent tool to have if you plan on making a lot of cuts, as it is designed to have spirit pass through its collection cylinder as it comes out below your condenser. The collection container of the parrot floats your proof and tralle hydrometer so you can keep an eye on exactly what proof is coming out of your still. The parrot empties into your collection or cuts jar (something shorter than it) via a spout.

> *Note:* **If you don't have a parrot, you can use a 250-milliliter glass test jar (cylinder) to measure your spirit as it comes out. Simply take samples from your collection jar and add them to your test jar and float your proof and tralle hydrometer to take readings.**

A **water source,** whether from a faucet or from a large vessel holding your cooling water, and a pump from your water source if not using tap water, is typically required of a still, as water is the primary way to cool a condenser. The related plastic or silicone tubing to connect to your condenser as well as clamps or barbs to keep the tubing in place is a requirement as well. A small tabletop still like the Still Spirits Air Still bypasses this and simply uses a fan for cooling, but most stills use some amount of water to cool.

A **heat source,** whether a gas burner, electric cooktop, electric element mounted inside the boiler, or induction heater, will also be needed. The heat source plus the need to be near a water source often sends distillers into the kitchen or garage, where both might be available.

> *Note:* **Traditional moonshiners or other remote and rural distillers may use a wood fire next to a stream or river, but both of those can be unpredictable sources of heating and cooling. Best to use modern conveniences if you have the option!**

From left to right (back to front): glass test jar, glass collection jug, different smaller foreshots jar, Grainfather G30 with alembic dome and condenser, condenser with collection tubing attached.

Optional but good to use, especially if you're filling your boiler to capacity, are **boil enhancers.** These help moderate your boil, keeping it even and avoiding boil overs or surge boiling. Boil enhancers are often sold as ceramic boiling chips. Any sort of small stainless, copper, or ceramic material will work, including rings that are sold for packing a still's column. Marbles or copper and stainless scrubbies can also do the job.

RUNNING A STILL

This tutorial assumes you have a well-built still with conventional parts in good working order. It assumes you're familiar with each part of your still as well. While every home still has a boiler and a condenser, how you heat that boiler and cool that condenser is up to you. Whether you're using a column and other related parts between the boiler and condenser is also up to you, but I assume you're running a pot still or have a column you understand how to use and manage, unless otherwise noted. There's more information on stills and their parts in Chapter 10. I will not be providing instructions that are better left to the instruction manual of your still (or a tutorial from the person who built it for you). What follows are the general instructions and methods you'll need to understand to take a wash and turn it into spirits, along with the best practices and tips that apply to most stills. (Most guidance in this book, including this section, refers to a 5-gallon (19-liter) batch size as well, as this is the most common batch size for home distilling.)

PREPARING THE STILL

Before you start, make sure the boiler is clean inside. Too much buildup may cause the boiler to corrode or heat unevenly. Prior to filling, you may want to add boiling chips, boil enhancers, pot scrubbers, marbles, or other material to the bottom of your still. You don't need to cover the entire bottom, as just a small handful gently spread out on the bottom will do the job. (I typically add 1 to 2 ounces of ceramic boil enhancers to the bottom of my 5-gallon boiler.) Having these materials at the bottom of your still will promote smaller bubble formation and decrease the chance of surge boiling of liquid through the still or sudden changes in temperature during boiling. They will also allow a more gentle and gradual boil without any expected temperature or pressure changes or surges.

(1) Most stills have separate boilers and domes that need to be attached. (2) Secure the dome as instructed by the manufacturer to avoid leaks. (3) Assemble the tubing on the condenser and from the collection end of the condenser, if needed. (4) Attach to cold water source or to a pump in water reservoir. (5) Be sure you're ready to collect spirits. (6) Adding ceramic boil enhancers can help provide a more consistent boil.

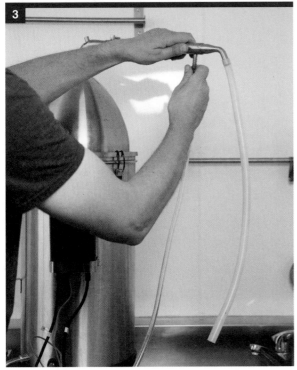

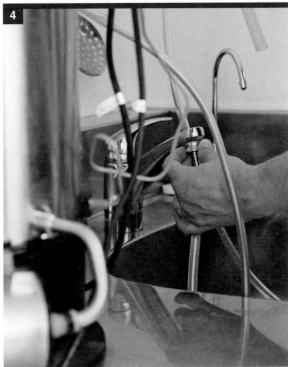

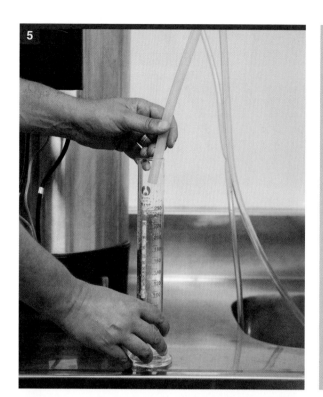

SURGE BOILING

Surge boiling typically happens when liquid becomes superheated (beyond its boiling point) and pressure builds up in the liquid. This pressure becomes volcanic as the liquid itself tries to push out of the still instead of becoming vapor. This is how some stills explode, though it usually only happens if a still becomes blocked and pressure can't release through the typical pathway out of the condenser. That's when the pressure decides to push on the sides of the boiler until it finds a way out.

FILLING THE STILL

Carefully siphon your wash or empty your wash through a spigot so as not to add too much solid material that has settled to the bottom of the fermenter. This mass of protein and yeast can gum up a still's operation, or scorch on the bottom of your boiler, creating uneven heat and off flavors. It's okay to leave a little wash behind. You'll want some free head space in your boiler anyway. (If you're typically going to make 5-gallon [19-liter] washes, you may want to consider a 7-gallon [27-liter] boiler.) A rule of thumb is to not fill past 80 percent of the capacity of your boiler. Your boiler needs room to manage small surges, and vapor pressure needs a chance to build prior to refluxing in a column or dome before reaching your condenser. There really isn't a good minimum volume I can recommend, but most people won't run a still until they have enough wash to fill it to at least 40 percent of capacity, for efficiency's sake.

Properly close up your still, as preventing leaks is critical. (There's nothing as disappointing as running a leaky still.) Whether you're using a column on a reflux still or an alembic dome on a pot still, confirm that it is well attached! Sometimes you don't notice until it's too late and you've lost a good amount of ethanol to the atmosphere. If you are using a column still, you'll also want to make sure your packing is clean and settled in the column. Be sure to follow instructions and be ready to stop the process and/or close off any leaks at the first sign of steam leaking anywhere. Steam is hotter than water, so be careful! It's always best to stop the distilling process before trying to fix anything.

You should have either your lid and column attached, or dome if using a pot still, and be ready to connect the condenser arm or flake stand (tub and coil condenser) if it's not already. If your condenser needs cooling water, be sure this is ready to go and appropriately connected to your still. If using a condenser arm, your water inlet is typically at the bottom end, farthest from your still, and the outlet is at the top, nearest where spirit would enter.

Let gravity do the work when filling the still if you have a spigot on the bottom of your fermenter.

Distilling conditioner is a surfactant, and can help prevent excess foam and wash coming through the still.

Place a jar or other clear container near the outlet and watch for vapor to begin to condense on it as heat is released from the condenser arm. (If you see this, you know something is coming out!) Some folks use their hands to check for vapor at the outlet, but I don't recommend it as this vapor is hot.

Soon after 145°F (63°C) you might see your still start to drip. Collect this condensed vapor, which is most likely methanol, until you have about 2 ounces (50 milliliters) and discard it. If you don't see any dripping until around 173°F (78°C), you may already be running ethanol and not methanol. However, you might be running both, as they like to bond together. This most often happens when the still comes up to temperature too fast, but since there's no easy way to check, go ahead and discard the first 2 ounces (50 milliliters) of foreshots—even if that's at 173°F (78°C), where ethanol begins to come through—just in case. It's best not to take any chances with methanol.

Depending on your decision as to whether you are going to run this particular batch of wash through the still once, twice, or potentially more times, follow the appropriate instructions on the following pages.

Now is the time to make sure the still is ready to condense from the start. Turn your boiler on and watch your column or dome temperature begin to rise. This is often referred to as the "head temperature", as it is taken at the head or top of the still (not to be confused with the first part of your run, which is called the "heads").

You don't need to run your condensing water at this time. If your still requires water to condense, as most stills do, you can generally wait until about 144°F (62°C) is reached on your head thermometer before you start to run your condensing water. At that point, begin to trickle the condensing water, waiting for signs of methanol to come through. (Some distillers wait until they see vapor coming out of the condenser before they turn their cooling water on, as they aren't concerned with condensing this first vapor because it's typically methanol.) Your still may also have come with specific instructions as to when to turn on your cooling water. If so, follow your still's recommendations.

A SINGLE RUN: COLLECTING HEADS, HEARTS, AND TAILS

As discussed, discard at least your first 2 ounces (50 milliliters) of the foreshots. Some distillers consider the foreshots to be the first 4 to 7 ounces (100 to 200 milliliters), as it contains both methanol and other alcohols that might not be useful, but it's ultimately up to you—some of the first 7 ounces (200 milliliters) can be saved and added to your next run. There is often some good alcohol that can be separated out in later runs, but for your own safety, you'll never want to keep the first 2 ounces (50 milliliters).

You'll want to keep your still running at a steadily increasing temperature, but slowly—otherwise you won't be able to make cuts. Fast versus slow is measured by how fast your spirit is coming out. If it's coming out in droplets, your still is going slow (potentially slower than it needs to be). If the spirit is forming a thin connected stream instead of drops, then your still is running at a good speed. Running slow and collecting droplets is fine, but your energy use to heat the still, water use to cool the condenser, and time will most likely not be maximized.

Once your speed is set, you'll be comfortable with the amount of heat being applied to the boiler and the amount of cooling water being applied to the condenser. Now you can focus on making your cuts. You'll run your still into a test jar or parrot. Typically, the cuts are then collected in numerous small jars. These jars can be divided into three major parts of your run:

1. **Heads:** Roughly the first 30 percent of your run. There is typically a strong paint-thinner flavor at the top of the heads, with lots of congeners. The heads can add depth when blending, but too much can make a batch taste strongly of alcohol and have excessive burn on the finish.

2. **Hearts:** The middle 40 percent of your run. The hearts will be mostly ethanol. It should smell neutral, alcoholic, and slightly sweet. Depending on how well your fermentation went, and how well you're running your still (make sure your boiler is still coming up slowly, and your condenser isn't getting too hot to the touch), you might collect something close to pure ethanol. The spirit coming out should be around 85 to 93 percent ABV if you're running a reflux still and around 60 to 80 percent ABV if you're running an alembic still.

3. **Tails:** The end of your run. This is defined by not a percentage of volume but when your alcohol gets below 60 percent ABV on a column still, or below 40 percent ABV on a pot still. Chances are you will find a lot of flavors here, which are rapidly changing as you collect. What you do with your tails, and when you stop collecting them, is up to you. If the aroma isn't great, it's probably time to stop collecting. If you're not sure when to stop, consider turning off your still by the time you begin running 20 percent ABV.

If your stream isn't consistent or becomes erratic, or you're seeing steam leave the unit as well as liquid, you're probably running too fast. You want the smallest stream of liquid possible for most stills and for most runs to be as effective as possible. Spirit being collected out of the still into a test jar for measuring the ABV.

Moving alcohol that's been checked for ABV to a cuts jar.

Note: If you're not familiar with your still or the recipe, you should try to segregate into smaller jars. You don't need to do this for the entirety of your run. Six 8-ounce (250-milliliter) jars for each for the heads and tails and eight for the hearts would mean twenty jars in total for a 5-gallon (19-liter) batch. That's a good start for learning a bit more than you would with ten jars. In return for this modest investment, you'll learn a lot about your spirit and your still. Smell and sip the various points of collection and you'll begin to pick up on the characteristics of each part of the run.

For a complete discussion of blending, see Chapter 6. For now, all you need to know is that heads and tails are generally not used in full quantities as they contain impurities, but they are added back in some quantity for flavor. Too much can lead to harsh or unwanted flavors and aromas. The right amount can give you something unique, complex, and lovely to drink. The more cuts you make, the more options you have when you're done—like a painter with a larger palette. This is the artistic side of distilling!

With the above in mind, you can take fractions or cuts as separate collections, generally every 17 ounces (500 milliliters) during a 5-gallon (19-liter) distillation process or run. Most folks focus on collecting about ten of these jars, roughly three for heads, four for hearts, and three for tails. More or less is okay. Some also choose to collect in much larger quantities, making three big cuts for heads, hearts, and tails. That's easier if you're planning a stripping run (discussed later) or know your still well enough to understand when the hearts start and end, as you want to avoid contaminating this middle part of the run. By collecting in smaller volumes, you will be able to blend your spirit from these separated cuts, choosing only the best-tasting jars.

DOUBLE DISTILLING: STRIPPING AND SPIRIT RUN

STRIPPING RUN

If you are running the wash more than once, you'll perform a stripping run as a first run, which means you can put the jars aside for now and collect everything that comes off your still in one vessel. Using two runs is done to help purify the alcohol a bit further. By performing a stripping run, you'll leave behind a bunch of congeners at the tail end of your run, and your second run should produce a much cleaner spirit.

You'll still want to remove the first 2 ounces (50 milliliters), the foreshots, on this first run. As mentioned earlier, some distillers remove 4 to 7 ounces (100 to 200 milliliters) of foreshots and heads knowing it will be quite estery and strong, as well as contain methanol. This spirit could be saved for another stripping run distillation, as ethanol and other congeners need to be further separated to be useful to your spirit run. After that, depending on the still and the product you make, you'll collect everything that comes out of the still for a while and then stop your stripping run when your still starts producing liquid at 40 percent ABV. (That is my recommendation as you get started, but as you gain experience you can experiment with going down all the way to 20 percent ABV, or consider using temperature as your guide and run your still until you reach around 208°F [98°C], at which point you've collected most good ethanol.)

SPIRIT RUN

Your second run (and any subsequent run, should you choose to repeat the process and triple or even quadruple distill) is referred to as a spirit run. Refer to the section on page 65 for a single run and follow the same rules around cuts, making them every 8 ounces (250 milliliters), and at a maximum every 16 ounces, and watching for a change in flavor and aroma between the first, second, and third parts of your run.

A parrot is a handy tool as it measures alcohol directly between the still and a cuts jar. This takes much less fuss than constantly filling and emptying a test jar to measure ABV.

Note: So your still runs appropriately and safely, you need to cut your alcohol to 35 percent ABV (a maximum of 40 percent ABV can be used) or the volatility of the alcohol and high vapor pressure may be an issue. The low boiling point of a higher-proof mixture will allow your still to move through cut temperatures quite quickly, and your cuts may blur, not allowing for a good, clean collection in the hearts. Also, alcohol above 40 percent has a low flashpoint; it's highly flammable, so heating this can be dangerous.

This spirit run can end when your still starts producing 40 percent ABV, or you can take it all the way down to 20 percent ABV, depending on what sort of flavors and aromas you're finding in your tails. Make your cuts and taste each jar before blending with it. It's up to you if you want to use the very end of this run or not. The main takeaway is that anything at 40 percent ABV or lower shouldn't be collected with your hearts until tasting, as the flavor can change quickly and dramatically.

POSTDISTILLATION

After distillation is complete and you've turned off your heat, you may continue to see liquid coming out of your still. This is to be expected: Your still is very hot and much continues to happen inside. Vapor is settling and heat is dissipating. Opening your still immediately following a distillation is a dangerous idea! Give it some time to cool down. If you know you can safely cool it down with a bit of water, feel free to do so, but keep in mind that vapor might be waiting for you on the inside. Clean up your boiler as soon as it has cooled, though, so you can be ready for another distillation as soon as you have a wash or run ready.

The remaining wash inside the still is called your backset. If at 20 percent ABV or less, it can be added to an active fermentation once cooled. If you don't have a fermentation going, store it in a sanitized container and freeze it if storing for more than a day or two. Without any yeast, it will attract bacteria and mold.

Clean your still very well. If there is any residue left by the backset in your still, there is a good chance you'll have mold in your still the next time you go to use it!

Copper sulfate is a byproduct of sulfur binding to copper and will be left behind on the internal copper parts of your still. Clean the inside of your still well in between runs. Sulfur is off flavor and off aroma in most spirits. Its ability to remove unwanted sulfur is partly why we use copper in stills.

POLISHING (FILTERING)
Chapter 4

Polishing, often referred to simply as filtering, is a common step after distillation, though it is one of the least discussed. In the home-distilling world, polishing is quite popular in countries where neutral spirits are preferred, either on their own or when infused with "spirit-style flavorings" postdistillation. Vodka is the most frequently filtered spirit, but it can be done across all styles of spirit.

A proper polishing of your spirit will have a positive effect on both the perceived flavor and aroma. If there were unwanted aromas present after distillation, the effect of polishing will most likely improve or remove them. For example, if you've added water and it was chlorinated, or not the best tasting, polishing can help improve the quality of your spirit by removing potential off flavors the water may have contributed, making its contribution more pleasant and neutral.

An important note before we begin: Polishing (filtering) with activated carbon doesn't remove methanol. If you forgot to remove the foreshots at the top of your distillation run, it's best to run your spirit through the still again.

Spirit filters come in various shapes and sizes. The stainless vertical filter, as well as the smaller carbon block filters, will all polish your spirit.

ACTIVATED CARBON

There are numerous filters for polishing a spirit, yet almost all are based on the use of activated carbon. Activated carbon is the most commonly used product for polishing spirits because it's effective and inexpensive. It removes the most volatile compounds and congeners in your spirit, the most aromatic substances that overshadow some of the more delicate grain or fruit notes you'd prefer to highlight.

Sometimes referred to as activated charcoal, or simply as charcoal, it is typically made using acids and chemicals, usually phosphoric acid, as well as high heat. The combination of the two during production creates the activation of the carbon, essentially eating away the material, creating lots of tiny holes. The base product is usually wood sawdust or wood chips. Plain old wood charcoal is often used commercially. A bunch of other products can be activated and carbonized though, including plastics, stones, coconuts, and other materials that can be burnt to a blackened crisp and made porous.

That last word is important: Activated carbon is extremely porous, giving it a large surface area for trapping larger impurities inside its pores. This is done through an attraction, or adherence, to the surface through adsorption by certain chemicals and compounds. This is different from absorption, in which molecules are incorporated or taken into a substance. Activated carbon is capable of this as well, but it's less likely during an alcohol polishing.

Activated carbon may be in a powder form, which can be tough to use at home. A granular or pelletized form is what you'll use on the home-distilling level. These may range in size from 0.25 millimeter to 2 millimeters. As all of these small granules can get the job done, it is up to the filter company or the end user to decide what works best with their equipment. (A common size found in the market is 1.5-millimeter granules, which seems to work with most filters.)

There are numerous grades and styles of activated carbon. What you must use is food-grade activated carbon. Typically, you can trust any activated carbon available from a home brew shop or distillation equipment and ingredient provider, but it might be worth checking to see if it's meant for a filter and for finishing a spirit. There are predistillation stage carbons out there that are meant for earlier in the process, during fermentation, as an extra safeguard against impurities created at that stage.

Loose carbon going into
a vertical filter—mostly.

Pore size varies greatly in activated carbon and matters more than the size of carbon you use. At a home-distilling level, it can be difficult to find this information because details about pore sizes often aren't published. Should you worry too much about it? I don't think so. Pore structure of commercially made activated carbon typically includes micropores and mesopores (large pores) and will capture small and large congeners. If your activated carbon isn't specific to distilling though, it may not be as efficient or safe to use.

Note: When made from peat, a preferred polishing carbon by many distillers, the carbon is sure to contain a variety of both large and small pores, able to capture impurities of all sizes.

THE LINCOLN COUNTY PROCESS

The Lincoln County Process is a unique charcoal filtering method that is a requirement in the state of Tennessee to make "Tennessee whiskey." Jack Daniel's distillery was the first to use this method of filtering for their whiskey. (Although some Kentucky distilleries also filter their bourbon, it isn't a requirement.) Typically, charred sugar maple trees are ground down to pellets or chips and added to deep vats with 135 to 140 proof whiskey. That whiskey is then slowly filtered out, sometimes over the course of a week!

Regarding the quantity to buy, I'd recommend a minimum of 8 grams of activated carbon for every 34 ounces (1 liter) of spirit you plan to clean. This would be considered a fairly "light touch" to the spirit. If you're doing a single pass through your filter over carbon, I recommend around 25 grams per 1 liter of alcohol as an efficient amount if used properly. This amount should not be overwhelmed by impurities and should thoroughly polish your spirit. Over 50 grams per liter will provide little difference and diminishing returns—not to say that you can't use more as a precaution. Thus, if cleaning 8 liters of newly distilled spirit, 400 grams is the amount you'll need. Of course, this is also assuming you properly run your filter and the spirit was adequately distilled.

You'll find most home-distillation filters may recommend adding more or less carbon than stated here. There's little harm in following their instructions; it may be the most effective way to use that particular filter. Also, some systems may have a minimum amount you need to fill them with activated carbon for the filter to work properly. Depending on their designed efficiencies, you could experience some spirit loss or less efficiency from your carbon than expected.

> *Note:* Polishing spirit can remove color. This is sometimes used intentionally for white whiskies and rums. These are often aged on oak and then the color, as well as a bit of flavor, is stripped away during the polishing process. Polishing to remove color can be a useful tool if you'd like to try make white spirits from an aged product.

LIGHT POLISHING: LEAVING A BIT OF THE "BAD STUFF" BEHIND

One aspect of filtering worth considering is intentionally not filtering your whole batch. You can perform a light polishing by partial batch filtering, intentionally using less carbon, or running your spirit through your filter faster. Why would you use this technique? During polishing we think of our congeners (fusel alcohols) as impurities. However, once we're to the aging stage, we think of them as potentially unique flavor compounds and characteristics of our dark (aged) spirits. During barrel- or oak-aging they become complex flavor providers. So maybe your fermentation created a larger amount of congeners than usual, but you're making a whiskey, rum, or other spirit that you'll be aging and want some congeners available for flavor development. By performing a light polishing, you'll leave some of the complex alcohols that develop your aged spirit's flavor over time.

CLEANING AND REUSING CARBON

Carbon can be cleaned for reuse by boiling and then baking the carbon until it's dry again. First boil your carbon in a pot of water that's at least twice as deep as the carbon for fifteen minutes.

After boiling, drain the carbon well and lay it out on a high-sided baking sheet, so it's no more than an inch deep. Apply 300°F (149°C) heat for three hours, stirring every five to ten minutes. This heating can also be done on a stovetop in a pan, but you'll need to be closely monitoring the carbon, stirring constantly, and keeping your heat low—a tough task for three hours! Either way, you should smell the ethanol evaporating away. Afterward, simply rinse the carbon with pure water as you would prior to your next use, and you'll have removed most congeners from the pores and brought your carbon back to life.

> *Note:* Remember that ethanol vapor is flammable, so running a fan is a good idea, as well as keeping any open flames well away from the tray.

If you're not in a rush to use it, you can let the carbon sit in a pot full of clean water at room temperature for several days prior to use for an extra bit of cleaning. Just pour off the water before using it.

This process is not as helpful for home distillers who send bad batches of homebrewed beer through their still to make whiskey or moonshine. (Yes, you can do that.) That's because there are numerous oils that can come through from the hops, as well as strange concentrations of fusel alcohols and substances from a batch of "off" beer.

Can you just purchase new carbon each time? Sure! Can you simply reuse used carbon after rinsing it? Usually! But, depending on how "dirty" your alcohol was, and how much carbon you used, its ability to polish might be limited. This is a hard thing to predict but easy to judge following a pass through the filter. The before and after will tell you how hard your activated carbon worked. (Just save a bit of unfiltered spirit to compare it to.)

DO I NEED TO POLISH MY SPIRIT RIGHT AWAY?

Nope! You can just store your clear spirit after distillation for filtering at a later date.

Also, it's worth noting that filtering can truly be performed at any point in the process. This might be post fermentation, or even post-aging, but it's going to be most effective and most predictable diluted with water to between 40 to 60 percent ABV unadulterated, postdistillation.

THE FILTER

Choosing the right filter for you will be primarily based on the volume of spirit you plan to filter after each batch. Match the size of the filter to your batch size and you'll have fewer problems. Follow the instructions provided with the filter, and if the filter is of good quality, you should have no problems and get great results! Still, if you want a little more info on filter types, here are a few of my notes.

CARBON BLOCK FILTER

A carbon block filter is a simple filter that has been designed for the home-distilling market. It's extremely popular for its size and ease of use. It uses a compressed block of activated carbon, meaning there's no loose carbon to manage. The density of the carbon block forces the spirit to pass through slowly. These systems provide good results overall, suitable for most folks looking to add a bit of polish to their spirit. As far as downsides go, consistency and quality of results can be an issue from time to time. Sometimes a second pass of the spirit through a carbon block can help.

CERAMIC FILTER

You may also come across home-distilling ceramic filters. These work pretty well, typically catching the largest impurities in your alcohol. The spirit should slowly move through the dense ceramic block filter before coming out filtered on the other side. If the spirit passes through the ceramic filter too fast, it won't effectively remove those nastier volatiles.

CONTAINER FILTER

One of the simplest ways to use carbon is to put it in a stainless or glass container and add carbon to it. That's it. Unlike a carbon block or ceramic filter, this is a somewhat passive way of picking up impurities. Stirring or mixing occasionally is necessary to get decent results. Most distillers choose to leave the carbon in a container with the spirit for two or three days, stirring whenever they get the chance. Just make sure the container can be sealed or you may lose more than expected to evaporation.

Note: For a container filter, carbon could be added loose if there's a drain that can be kept clear. Otherwise, you'll want to use a muslin bag or a fine mesh filter. Another possible way is to pass the spirit over filter paper, like a coffee filter.

VERTICAL FILTER

A vertical filter is an improvement on the simple container filter, as it features a long tube that holds carbon and a container at the top to hold the spirit. The spirit is then allowed to pass through the tube of carbon until it reaches a pinch point at the bottom, where there is a partially opened valve. Thus, the spirit is slowly but easily removed from the filter via gravity. The valve at the bottom lets you control the speed of release, allowing the spirit to slowly drip or run more quickly. Often, a large vertical filter allows you to use as little or as much carbon as you like without issue. In my opinion, this type of filter is one of the best ways to clean up your spirit.

Keep in mind there are other ways to polish spirits, but the general idea remains the same. The spirit needs to come into contact with activated carbon or be fed through something porous like a ceramic block. It then needs to be removed. It's as straightforward as that!

THE POLISHING PROCESS

This general tutorial is meant to cover some of the common processes and issues you'll encounter when filtering. For this example, I am using a vertical filter filled with loose carbon since it allows me to touch on additional topics, such as preparing the carbon. If you have a filter for home distilling that allows you to skip some steps in this tutorial, great!

CUT YOUR SPIRIT

Prior to starting the polishing process, you will need to dilute or "cut" your spirit if it is above 40 to 60 percent ABV. Using clean, filtered water, dilute your spirit to around 40 to 60 percent ABV.

Note: Don't dilute too much if you're unsure what your aging or bottling proof will be: It's pretty hard to take water out your spirit postdistillation! See the alcohol dilution formula (see page 94) as well as links to calculators online that can help. If you plan to age your spirit, you'll want to read ahead about aging (Chapter 5) to have an idea at what ABV percentage you'll want to age.

PREPARE YOUR CARBON

If you didn't buy your activated carbon from a home brew shop or from a store that understands your usage and the carbon it's selling, again, make sure it is food grade. You should consider boiling it before use. See the Cleaning Activated Carbon sidebar on page 81.

YOU WILL NEED:

- ▸ Spirit in need of polishing (at room temperature)

- ▸ Clean, filtered water (at room temperature) (Note: A carbon filter may remove some impurities from the water as well, but it will not be a miracle worker on poor quality water.)

- ▸ Loose activated carbon granules, from 0.25 mm to 2.0 mm in size (Note: Choose an appropriate amount of carbon for filtering. I recommend trying 25 grams per liter if you've decided to filter dark, soon to be aged, spirits, and around 50 grams per liter for clear and neutral spirits.)

- ▸ Filter (In the instructions to follow I'll assume it's a vertical filter filled with loose carbon.)

- ▸ Any other consumables (such as filter paper) or accessories (such as silicone tubing) the filter manufacturer may require

- ▸ Collection vessel, typically a glass jug or carboy that can fit the entire batch of the polished spirit

If you did buy your charcoal from a source selling it for home distilling, or once you've prepared your charcoal according to the sidebar note below, add the carbon to your filter and then add enough water to your filter to completely cover and soak your carbon. Let the water sit for at least 15 minutes (even overnight is fine). Agitate your carbon if it's easy for you to do with your filter. Drain off the water. Don't worry about the speed of draining right now; it can be as fast as your filter allows. You can repeat this step if you felt a lot of dust was removed from that first pass. If there was an oily film or white cloudiness to the water, definitely repeat the rinse, as chemicals from the carbonizing process were still present.

If you're using activated carbon that came in compressed blocks or cartridges for use with specific filtering systems, I recommend wetting these with water as well. These can either be rinsed or soaked, simply by setting them in water for at least 15 minutes or by passing water through them in their filter housing.

FILTER YOUR SPIRIT

Once the carbon has been rinsed, and the filter properly set up per the manufacturer's instructions, fill your carbon filter with your diluted spirit. It's best to let this alcohol completely saturate the loose carbon, so try to leave it in the filter for 24 hours or so before removing. Should you just run it through immediately the carbon will not have ample time to treat the spirit, and you may create channels in the carbon as well. It may just run down the edges of your wall if you're using a very fine granule of carbon, and it may not amply run through your carbon. A well-designed vertical filter will provide for great efficiency, but only if the spirit is allowed to completely saturate the carbon.

> *Note:* I recommend letting the spirit sit for at least 8 hours in the filter, but is 24 hours the maximum amount of time you should leave the spirit on the charcoal before running it off? Nope! Leaving it for days, maybe even a week, is not uncommon; there's no downside if you're not in a hurry. Just make sure your filter is sealed well, or you'll lose spirit to evaporation.

Once you're ready to run the spirit off the carbon, keep in mind that the speed at which you run off also has an impact on the effectiveness of the carbon. (If you filled your filter and all of your spirit is immediately in contact with carbon and left to sit in contact for some time—eight hours or so—the speed at which you run off will not matter.) I recommend a run off of spirit at around 2 liters per hour as a maximum. The other extreme is the tried-and-true slow drip, about one drop per second into a collection vessel. This is about as slow as you'd want to run off and works out to about 0.25 liters per hour.

Collecting around 1 liter per hour is a target for many polishers of spirit, and a great place to start. I find that two to four drips per second hits this mark. Effective, it is what most home distillers do. If you have a valve, just dial it back to the "break" in the stream where droplets come out. You don't want it flowing in one consistent channel of liquid; it should be breaking up and dripping as it leaves the valve.

When the drips completely stop, the polishing process is complete! If you aren't happy with the results, it's easy enough to run your spirit through again. Still not happy? It could be your carbon, your filter, or your filtering process, but the more likely culprit is that something is wrong with your spirit that polishing will not correct.

Once you've polished the spirit, make sure to completely close the collection vessel or move to containers that can be closed.

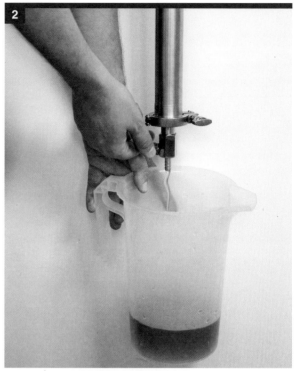

(1) Rinse your carbon with water by adding it directly to the filter. (2) Empty water from the still. Repeat if the water is quite dirty, as pictured. (3) Add the spirit to your filter. (4) Open the valve until you see 2 to 4 drips per second coming out.

CLEANING ACTIVATED CARBON

If your activated carbon is dusty or still seems to have particles stuck to it from the process of activated carbon creation, boiling the carbon in water before your first use is recommended.

To do this, add the carbon to a pot and top with water to twice the depth of the carbon layer. Bring the water to a boil and stir for fifteen seconds every two minutes. Keep this up for about fifteen minutes. Some folks will do this over and over until their boiled water is clear. With the carbons I've used, I've found once to be enough. Pour off the water and discard it. It's okay, good even, if the carbon is still wet going in your filter.

For improved cleaning and to dry for storage, strain the carbon from the water and spread out evenly on a baking sheet, no more than ½ inch deep. Bake at 300°F (150°C) for about 2 hours. Check the carbon and if some of the carbon is still wet, bake for an additional half hour. Remove from the oven and let cool before storing or using.

AGING (MATURATION)
Chapter 5

Aging spirits, or maturation, is a centuries-old tradition that you, as a home distiller, can continue. Aged spirits, sometimes called brown spirits, are quite easy to identify by their color, ranging from a blond yellow to a deep walnut brown. This is brought on by charred and burnt oak, usually from the inside of an oak barrel. Whiskeys, mezcals (like tequila), rums, and brandies are all commonly aged spirits, and the flavor complexity it brings can be unique and dynamic. If you're only interested in traditional gins and vodkas, or other clear spirits, the aging chapter is less necessary to understand.

BLENDING CUTS

Taking and blending cuts is really only necessary on your final run through the still. It's not necessary on your first run, your stripping run, unless that's also your last run. Whether you've segregated cuts into heads, hearts, and tails, or in even jars across the entire run, you'll want to start with the middle, the hearts of the run, and blend from the inside out. A few tips before we get started:

▸ To better understand some of the flavors, try diluting your spirit with equal parts clean water, which exposes some of the flavor notes that may be overpowered by alcohol.

▸ As you get used to this process, you'll be more likely to experiment and more likely to understand what you're looking for.

▸ Remember that if you're aging, some congeners can be your friend and some dynamic flavors and aromas are good, but nothing that comes across as harsh or offensive now is necessarily beneficial later.

▸ There's going to be trial and error when blending cuts, so be patient and take your time. Did I mention, don't be greedy? Your alcohol isn't going anywhere; you can recycle it in most cases (for more info, check out Following Up with a Feints Run on page 174 in Chapter 9).

▸ If you suspect things went horribly wrong or the results were not to your liking, you can still continue with aging and see how things mature. Or you can always redistill your alcohol.

YOU WILL NEED:

▸ Your jars of collected and numbered spirits

▸ 5-liter glass jug or jugs (or similar glass container to blend into)

▸ Unsalted soda crackers and clean water to cleanse the palate as needed

INSTRUCTIONS

When you make cuts, depending on the type of spirit you're making, feel free to go deep into the run. For rums and whiskeys that will be aged, you may want small amounts from each of your tails jars depending on how they smell and taste.

Have one large collection vessel handy to make your cuts into. If you have 15 even jars, I would number all jars from 1 to 15, and smell them as you go. If you're unsure, you may want to mark the first 4 as heads, the next 6 as hearts, and the final 5 as tails.

With the jars numbered, you'll likely want to start with 7. Hopefully, it tastes fairly clean, maybe a bit how you expected? It's not a bad idea to have sticky notes handy or a journal you can fill in as you take notes about flavor or aroma. You can pull up a flavor wheel to have in front of you, or take notes that make sense to you, even if it's just smiley or frowny faces and words like "Yuck!" or Paint thinner." Ethanol is slightly sweet, but the middle of your run may also have some of the qualities of your sugar base. I suspect this jar will be of a high quality and should be set aside to be added later. However, keep it handy as a comparison to other jars.

Now, compare it to jars 6 and 8. Which is more similar to jar 7? Focus on the one closest to 7. If it's identical in aroma and flavor, it should just be added to a larger blending vessel, one large enough to hold at least 60 percent of your cuts. If it's not, determine if you want to add the entirety (in most cases you'll want to).

(1) Check the aroma and taste. (2) Add spirits from jars to spirit vessel. (3) Write down any pertinent notes. (4) If you didn't do it during distillation, check the gravity of the jar. (5) The proof will begin to drop in your tails. (6) A spiral of toasted oak is added for aging.

From there, move to your third jar, either 6 or 8. Does it taste as expected? Close to the first two jars? Again, you'll probably want to add this entire jar to your blending vessel. If you're not sure, this might be a learning moment, or it might be a subpar run. You're in the middle of your run—all should be well with this jar. Set it aside for now and move on so you have another jar to compare the aroma and flavor to. Come back to it at the end, or after another jar if you've built confidence in the distillate it houses.

Based on what you discovered in your first three jars, maybe that jar 6 was quite clean and identical to 7, you may choose to go off toward your heads to see if you can find more of the good stuff: jar 5, then 4, then 3, and so on. It's not a bad idea to head in one direction or the other, and I recommend trying to move the direction that seemed to provide you with a cleaner, more neutral flavor. Otherwise, I prefer to continue with jars as close to the center of my run as possible, pulling jar 5 and jar 9 next. Give them both a good whiff. The less offensive one should be your next area of focus. Give it a taste. Most of the time, you'll notice a more dynamic flavor profile. If it seems inoffensive, it'd be a good idea to add the entirety of the jar to your blend.

The fourth jar, either 5 or 9, may start showing signs of congeners or acetaldehydes, likely in small amounts. If the flavor and aroma are inoffensive, adding the entirety of the jar is completely fine. If you're not sure, start by adding half of this jar to your blending vessel and set the other half aside. If you're looking to make this more educational, or want to take a repeatable or scientific approach, use your 250 ml glass test jar to measure out what you add in. Always measure your additions and mark them down if you'd like to better understand what parts of the run you favored. It'll be beneficial to review when you get to tasting the blend and the finished product.

Find jars 4 and 10: Jar 4 may be a mixture of heads and hearts, as jar 10 may be a mixture of hearts and tails. If you need to reset your nose, smell the back of your hand or your forearm. Too much alcohol vapor will start to burn out your sense of smell as well as your sense of taste. Resetting your nose, but also nibbling unsalted soda crackers and sipping clean water, will help reset your palette. If you're feeling fatigued, step away for a second or use your other senses. Dab your finger in the jar and rub them together to feel it. Does it feel oily? Give it a shake and look to see if it looks solvently or oily. Compare it to other jars. Be sure to take notes on what you observe. Everything from smell, touch, taste, and look can change from jar to jar.

As you did with jars 5 and 9, you'll want to start with the jar that was the least offensive. After jars 4 and 10, you have no reason to be greedy. I suspect the spirit currently in your collection vessel is quite good, and 25 percent of your jars is a great place to start if you think 4 and 10 may add some depth. There's no need to ruin this: All unused spirit can be recollected for another run! Keep a heads and tails (collectively referred to as feints) storage jug around. Blend these into your next run, or distill them completely separately for a wonderfully unique spirit!

Continue working your way through your final jars. These last jars (1–3 and 11–15) may provide nothing worth blending, or only small fractions of the cut. Take your time. When you believe you've finished, take your golden jar, jar 7, and add it into your collection vessel with the rest of your collected spirits. If you can, close the collection vessel and give it a couple shakes. If you can't close it, just give it a stir. Pour a bit out into a clean glass and check the aroma and flavor. Like it? Is it what you're looking for, whether that's ready to bottle and serve, or age, or infuse? If not, and you have a good memory or have taken good notes, maybe there's a jar out there that does. Add it in small amounts and smell and taste further.

AGING IN WOOD

Now that you've collected spirit, you may have made the decision to age it. In the case of whiskey, the decision is mostly made for you, or you'll drink unaged whiskey, which is moonshine. In the case of rum, brandy, or tequila, you may opt to age your spirit. Vodkas and gins are rarely aged, though there are distillers who have been aging gin, mostly as a challenge to the common practice of making a more neutral, clear spirit. Experimentation is the only way to get new flavors and new spirits, and it's great to see the tradition of aging as part of that innovation.

Congeners and esters, off flavors in clear spirits, are valuable harsh alcohols and compounds we're looking to tame during the aging process. It's interesting that something we hope to polish out of a gin or vodka is what we desire in our aged spirits. Consider this when making cuts from the still. These heavier alcohols contain immense amounts of flavor we want to develop, really break down, using a combination of charred or toasted wood and oxygen.

When we talk about aging spirits, we're referring specifically to wood aging. There may be other forms of aging spirits, but the goal in those is typically infusing or letting the spirit "rest," a settling of flavor, not dramatically changing the flavor through wood. Even more specifically, we are typically talking about using wood that's been toasted or charred. Most often this is carried out in wood barrels designed specifically for the aging of spirits.

The maturation process in barrels is a legal requirement of many spirits in many countries to be officially called by a specific name (whiskey), to receive an official geographic designation, or to uphold a "standard of identity," in legal speak. Scotch whiskey is a perfect example: It must be aged for three years. Aging makes a "brown spirit" that is dark colored, as opposed to "white spirit" that is typically clear and unaged.

A barrel thief ready to check what's inside.

Raw wood doesn't give spirit this color; the wood needs to be treated with heat, which means the barrel has either been charred or toasted. If it's been charred, it's a barrel that's been carbonized and blackened. This is pretty popular for dark brown spirits. Much like our activated carbon we use in the polishing process, a charred barrel can have the same effect, offering some polishing to the spirit. It also means that the sugars in the wood, hemicellulose, undergo a caramelization. A charred barrel will give you rich and round sweet flavors like toffee, caramel, and honey notes sought after in whiskey and other spirits. These sweet flavors create a much more smooth, mellow profile.

Some distillers may choose to use a toasted barrel, one that is colored but not blackened on the inside. This is a much gentler heat treatment than charring. It might not be fair to consider it a gentler aging on the spirit, though. There's a certain complexity to toasted woods that may not darken the spirit as much but can make it quite complex and lively. Depending on the level of toast, these barrels can create a wide range of flavors: vanilla, spices, toasted coconut, chocolate, coffee, and generally more woodiness (oakiness in the case of a traditional white oak barrel).

Left to right, top to bottom: proof and tralle hydrometer, glass test jar, glass jug, oak spirals or chips, and muslin cloth steeping bag for oak chips (optional).

WHAT YOU NEED TO AGE IN WOOD

Aging isn't difficult, and the list of required materials and equipment isn't very long. It's also pretty inexpensive if you avoid purchasing a barrel and just use other oak products. Here's a checklist to get you on your way to aging spirit:

▶ Appropriate barrel or between 4 and 32 ounces of oak chips, staves, or cubes

▶ Proof and tralle hydrometer (to help you determine your barrel proof)

▶ 250 ml glass test jar (to help you determine your barrel proof)

▶ Muslin cloth (or coffee filters)

▶ Glass aging and collection jars (if not using a barrel)

▶ A glass wine thief or stainless/copper barrel thief (for taking samples if using a barrel)

▶ Stainless racking cane and silicone tubing (for transfer if using a barrel)

▶ Stainless funnel (helpful when filling a barrel or filtering spirit off of oak chips)

White oak is preferred to any other wood for aging. It can be summed up in one word you'll rarely find a use for outside of nerdy discussions about wood: tylose. Tylose is a substance in wood that swells and seals the vascular structure or pores that would typically allow movement of water through wood. Tylose is an additional part of the cellular structure of white oak that many woods, including red oak, don't have. White oak is great for storage. Although evaporation will still take the "angel's share" of your spirit, it will be less costly to you than other woods might be.

Most European oak is grown in Spain. American white oak is quite widespread throughout the country. Through cost and accessibility, the majority of scotch produced is aged in American white oak. If you try scotch with strong notes of toffee and vanilla there's a good chance it was aged in American oak, which is naturally high in vanillin. If you find your scotch quite fruity, astringent, and dry on the finish, you're probably drinking a European oak-aged scotch. This is due to the higher tannin content in the wood. That said, European oak creates a certain depth or range of flavor and complexity that may not be achieved by American oak.

One aspect that's often overlooked by the home spirit crafter is the effect a barrel has through "breathing." Oxygen can reach the spirit through a wooden barrel and has a reactive effect on the alcohol inside. Oxygenation and esterification are both words used to describe this influence and change. Esterification refers to the chemical reactions with those congener alcohols and esters, a change to the complex molecules and compounds that are carried through from the still at the start and finish of your run. This change often allows other flavors to shine through, taking some of the harshness away from the spirit. It's not just the wood; it's these volatile compounds coming into contact with the air.

You'll hear a bit of talk about "terroir," a sense of place through the flavors conveyed in the spirit. Terroir goes beyond the ingredients used to make the spirit, and beyond the barrel, a reference to the conditions the barrel ages in. Many Scottish whiskey makers believe in being near the sea to have some of that saltiness imparted. Some bourbon makers believe cold winters, which shrink and dry the barrel, allowing more air to pass in, and more alcohol to evaporate out, is the only way to a rich, concentrated, dynamic flavor.

This brings me to the last key to maturation of spirits: evaporation. Much a part of oxygenation, air's access into the barrel and the alcohol's access to the atmosphere outside the barrel also exists. It's a two-way street. It's why most distillers refer to a barrel as something that breathes. Picture lungs expanding and contracting. Wood does the same thing with the changing of temperatures. I mentioned the "angel's share" earlier, which is the alcohol you lose when it's aging in a barrel. The average volume lost each year is typically around 2 percent. Wonder why that well-aged whiskey costs so much? It's not just the time involved but also the dwindling amount the distillery has left to sell—46 percent less spirit, possibly more!

CHAR LEVELS

Charring can be broken down into four levels based on time with an open flame:

LEVEL 1: Fifteen seconds of open flame applied. This is not a popular char level, though it can be asked for at a cooperage.

LEVEL 2: Thirty seconds of open flame applied. Although also not a very popular char level, level 2 is used by some distilleries to offer a potentially unique single barrel offering. It creates a nice sweetness; both vanilla and caramel can be dominant flavors in this range.

LEVEL 3: Thirty-five seconds of open flame is applied. I have now seen a cooperage that considers level 3 forty-five seconds of open flame. We're now getting into a level of char much more common in the whiskey industry. Caramel, burnt sugars, and much smoother spirit is produced at this level. The additional five to fifteen seconds truly darkens the barrels and the spirit significantly.

LEVEL 4: Fifty-five seconds of open flame is applied. Also known as the "alligator char," as the barrel takes on the appearance of alligator skin. Odd as it sounds, this char level doesn't exactly "lock in" the spirit but actually allows it to pass more easily to the wood, extracting more flavor from the raw wood and toasted parts. For that reason, many distillers prefer it for its complexity. The crackle of the charcoal layer lets the spirit enter the wood more easily as it begins to peel from the barrel. The peeling away also adds to more wood surface exposure, a bit of a win-win in the view of many a master distiller and blender.

*LEVEL 7: Not a truly identified char level, but an experiment at Buffalo Trace distillery has indicated that a level 7 char would be three and a half minutes of open flame. This goes well beyond alligator skin levels of char and has sparked conversations among home and commercial distillers about challenging what can be done with oak.

Although distilleries may be asking for barrels by char level, you can see that there are many changes between fifteen seconds and fifty-five seconds, and a range of seconds in there that aren't a predetermined char level. Typically specified by the distiller, these custom chars may also be used.

AGING YOUR SPIRIT

Let's make sure our collected alcohol is at the appropriate "barrel proof." Some industries, such as rum and whiskey, like to start using proof (which is double your ABV percentage) at this point in the process. Your proof should be between 100 proof (50 percent ABV) and 140 proof (70 percent ABV), which is a tried-and-true range. Can you use proofs outside this range? Sure. The latest data suggests the lower end of this is a great place to be, between 100 and 105 proof. Phenolic, harsh compounds break down more easily in water because they're water soluble. Oxidation of unwanted harsh compounds happens more easily with more water present as well.

You can find alcohol dilution calculators online, or if you have a large enough vessel, you can add clean water (distilled, spring, or from the faucet if there are no off flavors or aromas) directly to your spirit and use your proof and tralle hydrometer to determine when you've reached the proof you'd like to use for maturation. Another method is measuring out 100 milliliters of spirit and adding water to it until you're at the proof you'd like to age at in your sample. If you added 23 milliliters of water in your sample and have 1,000 milliliters of spirit in total, you'll add 230 milliliters minus the 23 milliliters you've already added to the 100 milliliters you pulled out, equaling 207 milliliters.

Again, this barrel proof you'll age your spirit at is a bit up to you. You typically don't add spirit in post-maturation unless you're blending from another barrel. Consider what proof you want to bottle and serve this at and be sure not to go any lower than that. You can always dilute further post maturation, which is pretty typical, as many spirits are right around 80 proof. "Cask strength" spirits are those bottled right from the barrel, with no further dilution.

One challenge to the home distiller is finding a barrel (or cask), new or used. Both exist and are available in most parts of the world. In places like the United States, France, and Scotland, where traditional barrel-aged spirits are made, finding a cooperage that can supply a new barrel, or a distillery or barrel broker that can provide a used barrel, shouldn't be a challenge.

Using a used barrel is a long-standing tradition in many parts of the spirits industry. It's not in the bourbon industry, which requires new barrels each time. For that reason, bourbon barrels move on to other parts of the industry: Scotland for scotch, the Caribbean for rum, and to Mexico for tequila. A barrel may stay in the industry for decades; it may be broken down and rebuilt, recharred, or retoasted. It might be used as is.

If you can get a barrel new from a cooperage, you might be able to pick your wood type, size, and amount of toast or char. If you go with a used barrel, try to source a fresh one. A barrel that hasn't been used recently and was left to sit unfilled will dry out and shrink. It's at risk of completely falling apart to loose staves.

However you source your barrel, make sure it's the right size for your needs, and use it sooner rather than later. Like I mentioned, a barrel likes to be wet. If you don't use it right away, it will dry out. If you're only able to fill the barrel half way, you may want to wet the top of your barrel down occasionally to keep it from shrinking too much during the aging process. Small rotations or rolling it (if it's a smaller barrel) will also help.

110 proof (55% ABV) is typical in the spirits industry for aging. 100 to 110 proof is a sweet spot for most aged spirits.

BARREL CARE

Barrels require some managing and care, but it's nothing that you can't handle. If you received a dry barrel from a distillery and don't plan to use it right away, you'll likely want to rehydrate it. Filling the barrel with hot water (whatever comes out of your faucet) right away is a good idea. It may leak, so do this outside or in a bathtub. If it leaked, wait twenty-four hours and wet the inside and outside of the barrel again. Do this each day until the barrel swells enough to hold water. Once your barrel is holding water, leave it for twenty-four hours, and then dump the water. The more time your barrel spends with water, the more likely you'll wash away the barrel's character, both toast and char, but also whatever spirit may have been present (should you want its influence on your spirit).

Need to keep it hydrated in the meantime? Add a small amount of your own alcohol, a couple of liters, or buy a cheap couple of liters of the same spirit you intend to add to the barrel. Close and roll the barrel so the spirit saturates and coats the inside of the wood. Roll the barrel occasionally, when you think of it, once a week at a minimum. The barrel might take in the majority of that spirit given time, and you may need to refresh the barrel until you're ready to fill it. Leave the spirit you added inside the barrel or remove it—you might find your barrel added more character to the cheaper spirit you purchased!

USING WOOD CHIPS, CUBES, AND STAVES

If you do have a challenge finding a barrel, there are a multitude of oak products available to the home distiller: oak chips, oak cubes, barrel oak chunks, oak spirals, oak staves, and any other small form toasted and charred oak can be sold in. I've seen Jack Daniel's barrels chipped for smokers; these can work for aging spirits as well!

You may want to experiment with different oak formats, materials, and chars or toasts. The beauty of using oak in these smaller formats is you can create your own custom blends in your aging vessel. I'd recommend you use multiple vessels with different oaks so that you can explore blending differently aged spirits together later on.

Standard glass jars or canning jars work well for aging. A wide opening is nice when using chips, cubes, or staves, so that you can easily add or remove them. Remember that the metal at the top might be reactive and rust, so shaking or filling to the top needs to be done with some caution. One thing you can do that more closely emulates a barrel is to leave the lid slightly open. I often put a small single layer of muslin cloth across the top and close the lid just barely finger tight. The cloth keeps the jar slightly open so the spirit can breathe. It's a great idea to find a way to let some oxygen in, even if it's just a tiny hole in your lid jar, to more closely mimic barrel aging.

Oak cubes, chips, and spirals can all be as effective as barrels for aging, if you use them properly.

Around an ounce of oak per quart of spirit works well, about 30 grams per liter. You can add more or less—this is your time to be artistic. More oak will age your spirit more quickly. Too much exposure to raw wood, which can happen with chips or staves, can add a strong woody or oak flavor. Add your oak in a muslin cloth tied shut, or simply raw. You'll want to strain your oak pieces through a cloth or paper coffee filter later on when bottling.

Woods other than white oak can be used for aging. Do a bit of research about a particular wood you might have an interest in to see if it makes sense for aging your spirit. You'll find many options: Almost all types of oak can be used; fruit and nut woods are popular as an alternative flavor source, providing their own unique character; ash, cedar, and alder all show up in distilleries from time to time as a unique offering.

So when is this maturation process done? That's up to you! The surface area that oak chips give you might mean after a few months your spirit is ready! If you're trying to be traditional, look up the rules and regulations for the type of spirit you're making, but be ready to age for three years or more if you're attempting to make a "true" scotch whiskey. I recommend occasionally tasting your spirit. I always taste my spirit after three months. In some cases, this is all the aging it needs, a general minimum for most aging. Six months, twelve months . . . the time starts to fly by. Nothing is stopping you from removing a portion of your spirit and enjoying it sooner rather than later, leaving the rest to sit longer.

If you've tied up your oak pieces in a muslin cloth, removal of the physical bit is easy. If not, take a couple standard paper coffee filters, or some folded muslin cloth, and set it over a jar. Press it into the opening slightly to make the material concave, so it is tucked inside the jar, hanging down an inch or so. If you can wrap the rest of the filter or muslin cloth over the edge of your jar and secure it with a rubber band, you can begin slowly pouring off your spirit. If you can leave oak behind, that's fine; if not, it should just fall into your filter material. Repeat as needed. You can enjoy it as is, out of the jar you transferred into if you like. If not, it's blending or bottling time!

If your spirit is coming out of a barrel, you'll need to use a barrel racking arm where the bung fits, or a stainless racking cane and silicone tubing to siphon. You may also have a spigot on the side, which makes things even easier. You might want to go directly into your final packaging from the barrel. If not, a glass wine thief or metal barrel thief is handy if you want to move a small amount of spirit into test jars for sampling and blending trials.

Let's move on to all of the other things you can do postdistillation and post-aging.

TOAST YOUR OWN CHIPS

Even if you've found toasted oak chips or cubes, maybe even used barrels that have been repurposed into chips, you might want to play with your own toasting. Perhaps you want to try out a different local indigenous hardwood. Simply take your chips, cubes, or staves and preheat your oven to around 400°F (205°C). Lay out the wood on a baking sheet, not too deep, maybe just a couple of layers at most. Place it in your oven, and after an hour check your chips (you can check earlier if they were already toasted). They should now be at a nice medium toast. You can play with temperatures: 300 to 350°F (149 to 177°C) will accentuate wood character; 350 to 400°F (177 to 205°C) will impart sweetness; 400 to 450°F (205 to 232°C) will add vanilla and toasted flavors; higher will achieve almondy and burnt sugars.

Raw chips can be checked throughout the toasting process to obtain light, medium, and dark toasts.

BLENDING, SENSORY, AND BOTTLING
Chapter 6

No matter what sort of spirit you make, there's always an opportunity for blending, something typically done after wood maturation. Blending is done between spirits of different strengths, different ages, from different types of barrels, and so on, creating something more complex, flavorful, and something completely different than achieved with a single spirit in a single barrel.

The hardest part about blending for the home distiller is having enough spirit around in a variety of aging stages or flavors to make it a valuable step. Blending is an art and science that requires a certain level of patience and practice to master. Most master blenders focus only on blending spirits, nothing else, and rely on years of hands-on study through apprenticeship under a master blender before they're allowed to practice their craft solo. You may decide not to use blending, which is completely fine. A lot of spirits, such as tequila, white rum, vodka, and gin, don't necessarily need any sort of blending or postdistillation infusion.

Sensory of your spirit is a critical component. What you think of it matters. You might be hard on yourself but try to give yourself some perspective. Compare it to your prior attempts. Compare it to commercial spirits. Take in feedback and take notes. Ultimately flavor matters. Let's adopt a subjective and objective approach to what you've worked hard at over the last weeks, months, and maybe even years to patiently wait to drink.

The final stage of distilling is the presentation of the spirit. You've put in the work to make a great spirit; now it's time to give it the right package. This can be as simple as an unmarked mason jar, or as elaborate as an ornate glass bottle with a cork and wax. Everyone from the backwoods moonshiner to the largest players in the spirits industry have known for a long time that the story you tell on the label (or with a lack of label), how you package your spirit, and how it's consumed change the drinker's perception of the flavor, quality, and value.

PREPARING TO BLEND SPIRITS

At this point in your journey, you probably have two or more spirits at hand. If not, and you only have one spirit aging, give it a check. Like it? Love it? It might be bound for bottling straight away. If you want to let it sit (or at least part of it) so you can experiment in the exciting world of blending, it's time to get another batch going. Do something different. Maybe the same recipe, but in a different barrel, or with a different wood chip. The difference in processes and age between your two spirits will be enough to allow you to start blending.

YOU WILL NEED:

- Two or more spirits in large enough volumes to blend with

- Unbleached paper coffee filters, funnel, and a glass test jar for filtering loose wood particles (optional)

- Glass or plastic wine thief or stainless sample thief (stainless baster or barrel thief) for pulling large samples from a barrel or large vessel

- 5 ml or 10 ml pipette (for smaller vessels and for precision when blending)

- Multiple 25 ml and 50 ml glass test jars to hold your samples (a cylinder or beaker works, one for each of your spirits)

- Wax or grease pencil that can mark glass to label samples

- Journal or paper for taking notes

- Tasting glass, like a Glencairn tasting glass or brandy snifter

- Distilled or spring water

- 100 ml graduated glass sample test jar for blending into (or a 50 ml test jar for small-batch quantities; a 250 ml test jar for numerous spirits or when tasters are helping with blending; or graduated glass beakers)

Water, a notebook, wine thief, and assorted glass test jars are the basics needed for blending finished spirits.

You'll soon find blending is one of the most critical tools in the distiller's toolbox. This is especially true of aged spirits, which can be blended as a mix of older and younger, even unaged spirits. Sure, single-barrel spirits can be quite unique, but often the hype behind these is primarily driven by marketing and scarcity. Is it the best spirit you'll ever drink? Probably not. It's there to provide a unique and different experience to the traditional stable of products a distillery releases. Blending is a tool that can increase the complexity of a spirit as long as you follow a few simple rules.

1. Never blend into a full batch without a trial on a smaller scale.

2. Understand what your different spirits offer and where their flaws lie, as well as their strong suits.

3. Flaws do not mean you're working with "bad" spirits. Never blend something you don't like into something you do. Think of blending as good becoming great, not bad becoming good. If there's an unwanted or offensive flavor, don't try to hide it through blending because you will probably not succeed.

BLENDING DIFFERENT SPIRIT TYPES

When we refer to blending, we're still typically referring to spirits bound to be the same final product. A whiskey with a whiskey, and rum with a rum. Blending is not confined to this norm, but you might find the blend of, say, a whiskey with a gin, something that may be a bit of a challenge to define and describe. The flavors that show up might be hard to wrap your palette around. Not to say it'll turn out poorly, but your brain does like to grasp what you're putting in your mouth, what it's tasting. If it's too challenging, it might suck all of the enjoyment out of drinking it. That said, a traditional genever, a Dutch spirit, is a blend of a grain-based "whiskey" and juniper-infused spirit. There are uncommon combinations that work.

FILTER AND PULL YOUR SAMPLES

Clear some space on a benchtop, countertop, or table to work. Plan on a specific blended benchtop batch size: 50 ml, or any number you please. For ease, I like working with 50 or 100 ml at a time, so I can easily do the math and determine the percentages of each spirit used later. If I'm working with say, three different whiskeys, and making a 50 ml blend, I'll take 50 ml samples out of each vessel. Measuring this sample out and looking back at what's left can confirm any sort of math in your blending jar later. Anything unused can always just go back in the vessel.

If you've aged with oak chips, spirals, or other types of loose oak, you may have a lot of wood particles in your spirit. This might also happen in new barrels with a strong char. One of the easiest ways to remove these charcoal dust and bits is with an unbleached paper coffee filter (or two if they're thin and prone to tear). Just place this inside a small funnel, similar in size to your coffee filter, and rest it on the top of a glass test jar. A plastic funnel is fine; if you're worried about leaching from the plastic, then use a stainless funnel. With this small amount of material, this process should take less than 10 minutes even if you are using a fine-tipped funnel. If your filtering stops, you can try slightly tipping your funnel a bit to see if it restarts or dump the contents back out and change your filter paper. If you're filtering a lot of spirit, a gallon or more, this might be tedious. Running your spirit multiple times through muslin cloth, something not as fine as coffee filter paper, may be faster.

As your samples are pulled, mark the sample jars with a wax or grease pencil. If you don't have one, use sticky notes, colored stickers, or something that can define each sample clearly. I typically number the samples and note them in my journal. Be cautious: You might remember now, but you haven't been sampling your spirits yet; your significant other hasn't asked you to mow the lawn; the dog hasn't started barking at the neighbor's cat . . . you get the picture. Blending requires focus, a well-organized space, labeled samples, and notes. It's also best to do this with your spirits at room temperature, as cold spirit can dull and mask aromas.

Once you're ready to proceed, it's time to move on to sensory evaluation.

SENSORY EVALUATION

Okay, it's time to get to know your samples. From your aging spirit, pull off 25 or 50 ml, or how much you think you'll need to get to know the spirit. Keep this in a marked test jar. You can also pull off additional amounts from your aging vessel into a larger marked glass test jar and a tasting glass at the same time.

In a tasting glass you might separate off 10 ml and add clean-tasting water to dilute the spirit. Doing this a drop of water at a time, nosing the glass after each drop, is a great way to get to know your spirit at different strengths. When performing sensory evaluation, some people even like to dilute the spirit all the way down to around 20 percent ABV. You can do this too if you like. My personal preference when blending whiskeys and rums is to dilute the individual spirits at first, adding about 10 ml of water to 10 ml of spirit by the end, which typically puts "barrel proof" or "cask proof"

spirit in the 25 to 30 percent range. The goal here is to allow the spirit to open up slowly, exposing itself and the different volatiles present. Ethanol and other volatile aromas can get in the way of aromatic nuances in your spirit. Dilution volatizes the aromas while in the spirit, settling compounds that were more reactive in the alcohol. Be sure you have enough spirit in your glass for a good spin around the bottom. This process of oxygenation may help wake up some aroma compounds inside the spirit.

While the spirit is still swirling in your glass, smell the spirit, bringing the glass up to your nose at an angle. This is referred to as nosing. Be sure to get the spirit close to your nose and don't be afraid to get your nose in there enough to pick up on what's going on. Everyone has a different sniffing and smell pattern but getting both short and long sniffs in is ideal.

Play around; figure out where the aromatics live in the glass and how best to get them across your nose so you can pick apart the scents into something discernable and communicable. Your nose will get overwhelmed by strong smells quite easily. Reset your nose by smelling your (hopefully somewhat clean and neutral-smelling) forearm or the back of your hand. Your nose is quite used to the smell of you, making it a neutral smell.

Next, take a small sip of the spirit. Let it slosh around your mouth, coating your entire palate from front to back and side to side, before you swallow, or spit, if you're likely to be sampling a lot of spirit (or have other things to do after sensory evaluation). Swallowing a small amount is the best way to understand a spirit's finish, but it's also easy to get lost in the sensory process and become more impaired than you suspect, so be cautious. Inebriation isn't great for making blending decisions, as your senses dull and your ability to make rational decisions goes downhill whether you like it or not. Put simply: You may make choices you regret later.

Let the flavor settle in your mouth. Breathe in and breathe out. Your sense of smell, and the aromatic effect, is always present and persistent when tasting spirits and will deliver to your brain what it suspects you should taste. Following a small swallow or spit of alcohol, the spirit may present something different. What's registering at this point is technically still aromatics but those that are left coating your mouth and throat. These might be different from what was present early on. Process what you just nosed and tasted, and what the aftertaste is. Take plenty of notes.

If your mouth and brain are feeling a bit overwhelmed trying to process what you just tasted, you may want to consider having clean, cold water around, as well as unsalted soda crackers, to reset your palate. Ethanol and all of those flavors can do a number on your taste buds. It's also reasonable to take a break and come back to it.

When taking notes, you can separate aroma and flavor if you like or combine both into your journaling of the process. If something is, say, fruity, this is a fairly general descriptor, and you may make this a topical or headline sensory note, and then see if you can dig deeper, getting as specific as possible. It's great to understand what fruit flavors you suspect to come across in your spirits as certain fruits are quite typical of certain spirits. It's also good to have worked your way through as many of those different fruits as you can over the course of your life, as it's hard to describe something as dried apricot or fresh lychee if you've never tried one.

From there I personally like to use "slightly" or "very," abbreviated SL or V, respectively, in my notes. This gives me a quick way to mark down more than just what I taste or smell, using a weighted scale. For example, "SL cooked corn," "cooked corn," or "V cooked corn." Another option is to jot down flavors and aromas as quickly as possible, and then go back and weight these using numbers, maybe using a 1 to 3 or 1 to 5 scale, with the largest number being a stronger character. Beyond this, if it's a flavor or aroma you appreciate, you may want to highlight or put a star next to this attribute. Maybe this is a nice toffee note in an aged rum that you really enjoy. On the opposite side of this coin, you may want to note strong offensive flavors and aromas, or flavors you don't want to be too obtrusive in your final blend.

Note: **Having a flavor and aroma wheel, chart, or table in front of you is a great way to start learning what to look for in your spirit. It's not cheating: It takes time to commit many of these flavors and aromas to memory through both memorization and practice, as well as expanding your palate.**

SENSORY GLASSWARE

There are a variety of glass styles you can use for sensory evaluation. Some are branded and built for purpose, and others may be more general, originally designed to enjoy a bottled spirit (or something else entirely). Any glass can be used for sensory or sipping, but some offer advantages that may make a difference for you.

NOSING GLASS: Generally, a nosing glass is what you'll most often see at whiskey tastings and around whiskey labs at distilleries. Most large glass companies, including Glencairn Crystal and Riedel, manufacture this glassware. It may also be known as a Glencairn glass, as they have popularized the style and done well to promote it. The bulbous bottom end and slope inward midway up the glass allows the distiller to get to know the aromas quite quickly as they condense inside before reaching the rim. It makes for a big aromatic effect when you get your nose down in there: Be ready!

BRANDY SNIFTER: A brandy snifter comprises many elements of a good nosing and tasting glass. A bulbous form allows volatiles to swirl in the glass, and for many to be captured and held inside the turned-in lip. Just be sure it's not so big that you can't get your nose down near the spirit for a good whiff (or be sure to use enough spirit).

TULIP GLASS: Somewhere between a Glencairn-style nosing glass and a brandy snifter lies an assortment of tulip glasses. Short or long stemmed, these glasses have the curvature of a good tasting glass and are often a nice size for sampling and sensory purposes. A cognac tulip or stemmed whiskey snifter, sometimes called a copita, is similar in shape to a nosing glass, and is appropriate for most spirit sensory.

THE NORLAN: This is a unique, double-walled glass that the manufacturer says is made with two separate molds. Is this valuable? I'm not sure, though it is more than suitable for nosing, sporting a cool "hybrid-tumbler-nosing glass" look. It's designed for a more diffuse approach to aromatic sensory, which may allow some of the more delicate aromas hidden beneath the ethanol to come through.

THE NEAT: An acronym for "Naturally Engineered Aroma Technology," the NEAT tasting glass cuts down on ethanol aromas, but possibly not as much as The Norlan. The glass has started to earn quite a following and has become an industry standard at numerous whiskey competitions. With a wider opening than a Glencairn, the glass lets more ethanol be released prior to assessing aroma, but it also uses a turn-in prior to the lip to help trap and condense some of those volatiles before they escape. A wide lip allows the entire spirit to coat your mouth and cross your palate when tasting. Having used this glass, I feel it's an excellent go-to choice across all types of spirits.

THE D&L: The Denver & Liely whisky glass is worth a mention as it offers a blend of snifter and tumbler. D&L believes they've created both a high-end everyday glass, as well as a sensory tool. I can't speak to this glass personally, but it looks great and might be the perfect choice for you if you are mostly working on whiskey.

A Glencairn glass ready for some sensory.

MAKING BLENDING DECISIONS

Once you've gotten to know your blending components, it's time to take an objective look at what you've uncovered through sensory evaluation. Are there similarities between the spirits you're blending? Do all of the spirits have a vanilla note to them? If so, you know this will be a constant in your spirit and something to balance against. Now take a subjective look. If there were some highlights you marked down for your spirits, attributes you want in the final blended spirit, make sure you choose that spirit as a major component of the blend. Were there any harsh or offensive flavors you want to avoid? Make sure to limit or omit that spirit from the blend.

To start a blend, take a 50 ml or 100 ml testing jar, something you can accurately measure in, and begin by adding your base spirit, the one you plan to use the most. This is a bit of a guessing game, but you'll need to start somewhere: I like to add 15 to 20 ml of this spirit, depending on my confidence, assuming I have at least two or three more spirits to blend in. With a goal of 25 ml in total for the final blend, I'll then add around 5 ml of the other spirits, noting precisely what I did. Once I have my 25 ml of blended spirit, I dump half of this blend into my tasting glass. You can follow this exact formula or a variation of it, of course.

Good organization and labeling is necessary when blending multiple spirits.

Swirl or stir the spirit so it blends together. Time for more sensory: Starting with the aroma and moving on to taste, take notes as to what aromas and flavors you're getting. Is it meeting your expectations? Are the highlights from the previous spirits coming through? Are you getting the nuances you want? Is anything sticking out you don't want? Look back and see where it might be coming from.

Continue by diluting your blend as you taste by adding drops of water to your glass. You'll want to do this especially if the final product is meant to be bottled at a lower proof. You can roughly calculate and measure how much water is needed to create a "bottle proof" version of your "barrel proof" in your test jar as well and start there, if preferred. An additional 9 ml of water will take a 55% ABV spirit down to 40%.

Keep the remainder that blend segregated, and start over in a new vessel, again aiming for 25 ml (or the same volume as before). In this second blend, use your notes from the first blend and try to optimize/dial in. Or, if you did not enjoy your first blend, you may change it more radically. Continue through this process as many times as you like, making notes about your blends and the sensory. You might find you go back to an earlier blend to compare the aroma and flavor, and after a few different blends, make the decision that your first blend was the best.

Here's an example of a whiskey I blended recently, and my notes transposed verbatim:

55% ABV "Single Malt Experiment" 9 Months—American charred oak spiral 8", copper column still, hearts only, single run, 450 ml	55% Experiment' 6 Months—American charred oak spiral 8", air still, hearts only, single run, 400 ml ABV "Single Malt"	50% ABV, 2 years dark toast oak chips (not measured), malt extract, Grainfather alembic, 600 ml

AROMA
▶ Sweet, dark fruits
  • SL Prune
  • Raisin
▶ SL Wood Smoke
▶ Stone fruit
  • Ripe Plum
 	
FLAVOR
▶ V Smokey
  • Campfire—too much oak for quantity of spirit!
  • Also some SL Raw Wood flavor
▶ SL Caramel finish
▶ Tobacco
▶ SL Coffee
▶ Leathery
	AROMA
	▶ Sweet
	  • Toffee
	  • Vanilla
	▶ SL spicy, pepper*
	▶ SL chocolate
	Nice aroma!
	
	FLAVOR
	▶ Smoke—less so than same wash at 9 months age (diff. still.)
	▶ Toffee*
	▶ SL Burnt Sugar
	▶ Grain
	  • Malt*
	  • SL Malted Milk
	  • Fresh, green, SL astringent cereal
	  • Grape nuts
		AROMA
		▶ Vanilla
		▶ SL Honey
		Somewhat dull, one dimensional.
		
		FLAVOR
		▶ V Vanilla
		▶ SL Burnt Toast
		▶ SL Molasses?
		▶ Malty—sweet grain
		▶ SL Fruit Cake—dried sweet fruits, prune, orange, with slight spicy, "Christmas blend" note

Blend #1 5 ml	Blend #1 15 ml	Blend #1 5 ml
Blend #1: Smokey, dark flavors still too much. Nice complexity. More of oldest?		
Blend #2 2 ml	Blend #2 15 ml	Blend #1 8 ml
Blend #2: Nice. Improves "6 month" base spirit. Dropped ice cube in; opened up nicely.		
Could maybe just blend air still with 2 yr, 50/50? Will keep as is, #2. **Final @ 100 ml—9 mo @ 8%, 6 mo at 60%, 2 yr @ 32%.** **Final] 6: 9 mo 48 ml, 6 mo 300 ml, 2 yr 192 ml = 540 ml barrel proof, diluted to 40% w/ 180 ml = 720 ml**		

Once you've found your perfect blend, do a bit of math to determine which spirit in your blend will be the limiting factor in production volume if it still makes logical sense to bottle the blend. In most cases it's best to not make this the determining factor; you want to blend to make the best spirit possible, not to use up spirit. This might mean you only get one bottle of finished spirit. If you look at my note around the final quantity I collected and blended, you'll see I adjusted up to 100 ml first, an even number from which I could glean percentages. I ended up with 540 ml total. After tasting and blending, this was near the limit of what was possible, based on the amount of my base spirit (the 6-month-old) I still had on hand. I ended up putting this blend in a 500 ml bottle and enjoying my extra 40 ml of it that day!

DILUTE YOUR BLENDED SPIRIT

Following this you'll dilute your blended spirit to your finishing strength, your bottled strength. This is yet another area for you to be a bit artistic with your spirit. Sure, most whiskeys, rums, and gins are diluted to 40 percent, but not all. Look back at your notes from dilution; there may be some hints on where to start. If you dilute your blend slowly (if at all) or take measured samples of your blend and add varying amounts of clean water to them to compare different proofs, you'll find that your spirit has a different flavor at 50 percent ABV (100 proof), 45 percent ABV (90 proof), and 40 percent ABV (80 proof). Don't be afraid to find where your spirit wants to live and with what you're most happy. Most commercial distillers who are not making a sugary liqueur will tell you anything below 38 percent ABV (76 proof) starts to get a bit of a "watery" note and mouthfeel to it. Anything above

65 percent ABV (130 proof), even a rich complex spirit, is often overwhelmed by strong alcohol aroma and flavor. Still, a 38 to 65 percent ABV for most common clear and aged spirits is quite a large window to work in.

The process of blending can be a rewarding step in the distilling process. It's yet another creative lever we get to pull when making spirit. If you're feeling frustrated, indecisive, or nervous you might ruin the hard work you've put in up to this point, take a step back, take a deep breath, and remember it's just spirits. And you're blending in small quantities first to make sure you avoid bigger mistakes later, so the risk is low. Let good note taking and your own flavor preferences and palate be your guide.

BOTTLING SPIRITS

Once you have your spirit ready for the bottle, whether blended or direct from the barrel, it's important to give it a presentation you're happy with. Take a look at the types of bottles and closures that are often used for the spirit you're making. Sourcing similar bottles, or even reusing commercial bottles, may be the way to go.

Size is one consideration. Spirit bottles are available in various shapes and sizes, down to 50 milliliters (if you like to pretend you're on a plane or in a hotel) and up to 5 liters, if you'd prefer to bottle in bulk. Throughout the world, 500 milliliters, 750 milliliters, and 1 liter are the most common, though of course glass jars (like canning jars) are common among home distillers and moonshiners as well.

If you choose to go with glass bottles, all you'll need to transfer is a small funnel to help you fill your bottles. There are plastic and stainless bottle fillers and siphons designed to do the same job, but these only make sense if you're mass producing your spirit, putting it into multiple bottles (maybe more than a couple of dozen), and bottling off a large vessel. Unlike home brewing lower alcohol beverages, such as beer, there is no need for sanitizing solutions or equipment, though you do need your bottles to be clean.

If your spirit is in a barrel that doesn't have a tap, you can empty it into something that is easier to pour from, such as a glass or stainless pitcher. If the barrel is too heavy to move, consider a racking cane, which is just a solid tube with some tubing attached to it, to help you siphon from the larger vessel without having to pick it up or move it. There are also more complex racking canes, called autosiphons, that allow you to pump start your siphon first. Easy to use, they can be great if you're struggling to get a siphon going from one higher vessel to a lower vessel.

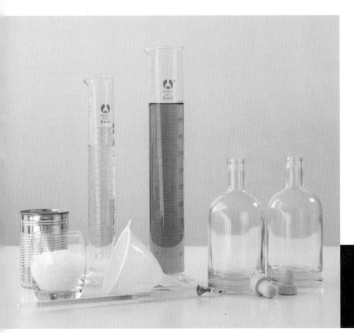

Left to right: tin can, wax beads, glass test jars, funnel, proof and tralle hydrometer, bottles, and corks

CORKS, CAPS, AND LABELS

Most cork-finished spirits use a T-cork, or similar flared cork, to make uncorking easy. Unlike a wine bottle, there's a good chance you won't be drinking the bottle all in one sitting, so you want a finish like a T-cork that you can easily put back in and remove again. A T-cork may have a PVC shrink capsule applied over it, or it may be waxed. Some may just have a piece of decorative tape over the top with the spirit or spirit company's name.

Becoming more popular with home distillers, as it already is with the largest commercial distillers, are twist caps. Easy to open and close for the drinker, these metal caps fit snug on threaded bottles and work well as a simple way to finish a bottle. Some of these caps may have a shrink capsule over them, while others tear away from a foil neck. If you're reusing a major distiller's bottle, it's likely the cap is threaded. These will work fine for your spirit.

Labelling can be anything from a bespoke label designed on your computer to permanent marker on duct tape! Either way, make sure it fits the look and feel of the spirit inside. People drink with their eyes, which includes the impact of the bottle and label. On the label, consider including key information such as spirit type, proof, and bottling date.

Most spirits can be stored for years, even decades, as long as there are no fresh ingredients or other additives that may spoil (for instance, if you bottled your gin with fresh berries). With a proper seal, the spirit won't escape the bottle and you'll be able to enjoy it tomorrow or years from now. As you enjoy the spirit, more oxygen will be introduced and may have an effect on the flavor—especially on those that were aged. That's okay! Spirit is meant to change as it ages and, in most cases, it will provide the drinker with a new and exciting experience each time.

Corks and screw caps come in a wide variety of shapes and sizes. Find what works for your bottle and your spirit.

HOW TO WAX SEAL

One of the most popular ways to finish a spirit bottle is with wax, which creates an excellent barrier from oxygen and the environment. Your spirit will likely want to slowly evaporate away, and a good waxing on top of your corked bottle will complete the process and protect the spirit. Bottling wax or sealing wax only needs to be melted to be used. Bottling wax often comes in small beads that are easy to melt. A single 1-pound (0.5-kilogram) bag of wax beads should have no problem sealing upward of fifty bottles. You often have your choice of color: Reds, blacks, and whites seem to be the most common. You might find white wax and powdered colored dyes that can be mixed in as well, like that pictured.

If I'm only sealing a few bottles, I prefer to use a small- or medium-sized standard soup can filled about half full of bottling wax. Be sure to take the label off, as we don't need any accidental fires during bottling! Whatever can size you use, be sure you can fit the neck of your finished (corked) bottle down into it. A smaller can will waste less wax, though you can let the wax harden in the can and use it again.

Fill the can about two-thirds of the way full with wax and apply medium heat to the can. If you have colored dye to add, you may add it now. To be safe, you may want to set the can in a shallow pan with ½ inch or more of water in it to act as a buffer and double boiler. This will melt the wax more uniformly. Using a wooden ladle handle or a chopstick, stir slowly until all of the beads have melted. Don't use plastic utensils to stir because they may melt. Metal utensils may melt as well, and you may be working to get wax off of it for quite some time.

Once the wax is melted, take your spirit bottle and dip it in the wax, making sure the entirety of the cork and part of the neck is covered, all the way around. Lift up carefully; wax will begin running down the bottle neck, giving you that handcrafted look. Once dried, you can dip the bottle a second time if you'd like more wax. Or, if you have additional wax at the end, you may want to carefully pour a bit over the top for effect. You can even buy or make a small stamp for a unique flare on top. There's little else you need to do. If your first bottle wasn't waxed completely, or you'd like more depth of wax on the neck, simply throw in some more beads and melt them. It's much easier to adjust the height of the wax inside a smaller hot wax can. Just be careful: You'll displace the wax as you dip the bottle, so be sure not to fill the can so high that it overflows.

VODKA, GIN, SCHNAPPS, AND BEGINNER-FRIENDLY RECIPES

Chapter 7

Many spirits, including vodka, gin, and schnapps, can be made from nearly any type of sugar base: grains, sugar cane, and molasses, but also fruits, vegetables, and really any other sugar source, natural or refined. What's more, the initial recipe for each of these unique spirits might be exactly the same. Because this sounds quite vague, you may question what actually defines spirits like vodka, gin, and schnapps.

So, let's start with a generalization of all spirits: If you've made alcohol for the purpose of consuming and it's been distilled, you've concentrated alcohol, and it's a spirit! How that spirit is further treated, and flavored (or not), starts to define what it is. It can go beyond what base ingredient you use. It also depends on how you distill it, how you treat it after it comes out of the still, how it tastes, and, if we want to get technical, where you reside when you make it.

As home distillers we typically don't worry about the whole geographical issue because we're not putting a commercial product on the shelf. If we make something with blue agave syrup, we'll probably call it tequila, even though we don't reside in Jalisco, Mexico, a requirement to call something tequila instead of the more general "blue agave spirit." To better wrap your head around it, see the Geography row in the table on page 126.

WAYS WE DEFINE SPECIFIC STYLES OF SPIRITS	UNIQUE SPECIFICATION	SPIRIT EXAMPLE
Ingredients: The specific ingredient used is the most common way to identify a type of spirit.	▸ Barley ▸ Grapes ▸ Cane sugar ▸ Molasses	▸ Whiskey ▸ Brandy ▸ Cachaça ▸ Rum
Process and equipment: The process changes from spirit to spirit, and for some spirits is a legal requirement for a spirit to be "defined" as such.	▸ Type of still ▸ Filtration ▸ Aging ▸ Infusions	▸ A column still for vodka ▸ With charcoal for Tennessee bourbon ▸ In barrels like whiskey ▸ Adding botanicals like juniper to gin
Flavor: Although a spirit category may be quite diverse, there are usually defining flavors that help us identify a spirit.	▸ Peat smoke ▸ Herbal ▸ Toasted sugar ▸ Floral	▸ Scotch whisky ▸ Tequila ▸ Rum ▸ Cognac
Geography: Geographical indications (GIs) or designation of origins (DOs) are often used to identify a locally produced spirit, allowing for unique labeling names and claims, but also may create confusion as a common spirit produced outside its traditional country or area in the same way may need to go by a completely different name.	▸ Tequila ▸ Armagnac ▸ Bourbon whiskey ▸ Pisco	▸ Parts of Mexico ▸ Parts of France ▸ United States ▸ Peru

So why doesn't the base ingredient matter as much in the spirits we're talking about in this chapter? In vodka, it's because part of the goal is to create a somewhat neutral, clean ethanol character. Gin takes this one step further and infuses botanicals during distillation into the neutral spirit to create a unique and complex, juniper-driven spirit. Schnapps takes that same neutral spirit and heavily infuses it postdistillation with whatever you like (though traditionally, it's with fruit or herbs and sweetened with sugar). There's also no geographic designation for calling something vodka, gin, or schnapps.

VODKA

Early vodkas were likely made from grapes, something that was already being fermented in monasteries by monks. As early as the eighth century, some rough form of vodka was being produced in the areas that would become the western Slavic countries, including Poland and Slovakia. Over the course of the next 600 years, the making of vodka spread across Europe and made its way to Russia, where "aqua vitae" (the general name for most distilled products back then) was widely traded.

By the fourteenth century, most vodka was still being made on alembic pot stills, reflux wasn't well understood, and it's thought most vodkas were being distilled two to three times to reach a collected spirit of around 70 to 80 percent ABV. This would then be watered down to anything from 30 to 40 percent ABV. It wasn't until the 1800s, when Napoleon challenged France to become more self-reliant, that sugar beets came into the picture.

Although vodka is quite neutral, that doesn't mean it's flavorless. What it does mean is that ethanol is the dominant flavor, and there may be subtle hints of the base sugar that linger on the nose or the back of the palate. If you've had at least two different types of vodka, you probably know they're not all the same.

GIN

Much like vodka, monks had their hand in the origins of gin. It's thought that Italy, a place not closely associated with gin these days, was its birthplace in the eleventh century. Over time, Holland popularized it and Britain modernized it.

Why throw juniper berries in a spirit? That may be the central question for gin, which is to this day generally associated with juniper. Like many beverages throughout history, both alcoholic and nonalcoholic, botanicals such as juniper were originally added for medicinal purposes. Juniper eventually became a popular addition to aqua vitae, or vodka, for another reason as well: Since distilling was still quite rustic and the spirits not all that palatable, juniper could be used to cover up those nasty congeners. Sometimes distillers would use a large amount of sweet or strong botanicals (think licorice root) as well as sugar to cover these up. It made these gins quite dynamic, sweet, strong in flavor, and heavy on the palate.

Gin eventually developed into what we know today as gin, which is to say a typically neutral spirit with juniper, a requirement, as well as a wide-ranging assortment of botanicals to suit different tastes. London Dry has been the most popular style of gin for quite some time, though even within that style flavors can be wide ranging these days.

Dry gin was initially used to define a gin that had been made from a clean neutral spirit, not one poorly made on a pot still containing off flavors and congeners. While botanicals were good at covering these up, there were typically signs in the aroma and finish that impurities lived on in pot still gins. Dry gin, on the other hand, was made on the newer Coffey column stills, which resulted in a high-quality, clean spirit. It was smooth on the palate, not overbearing, and finished neat and clean (hence, "dry"). The only aromatics were those of pure ethanol and the botanicals. London Dry (and other British) gin drinkers made juniper the star, though most makers weren't afraid to go another five to ten botanicals deep in their gin baskets. Although the gin itself often wasn't made in London, it was mostly made for London's refined gin palates during the 1850s, and so the spirit gained the moniker of London Dry gin.

The London Dry style is still the benchmark for quality gin and requires a distiller to focus on both their distillation techniques as well as their botanical infusion balance. Juniper is still a legal requirement in some countries for gin, and most modern London Dry gins also contain some six to nine other botanicals: almost always coriander and angelica root, possibly some citrus peel from lemon or orange, and probably a spicy note from cinnamon or cassia.

Other popular styles of gin besides London Dry include the following:

Genever: Also known as jenever, this is the oldest of the modern gin styles. It's Dutch and typically made only in Holland or Belgium. Often it's a blend of two separate spirits. One is a "malt wine," essentially a neutral spirit made from grain, often malt, corn, and rye, which is aged. Then using part of this malt wine or another neutral spirit, another distillation with a juniper-forward blend of botanicals is performed. This is then blended back into the malt wine. Because of the blending with aged spirit, genever may have a bit of color and a bit less dominant botanical flavor.

Old Tom: At one point, this was the antithesis of London Dry gins, and not in a good way. However, distilleries have embraced it and made a nice, warm, well-rounded gin these days. It's meant to be sweeter, with much less juniper and often a lot more licorice. It may have sugar added, and some examples of this style may even be aged on oak, which will bring out different sweet caramel and vanilla notes from the barrel. Some distillers have really started playing with the style, creating unique, full-bodied gins that offer something interesting and quite enjoyable as a change-up in classic gin cocktails, like a Negroni or Tom Collins.

New American: This would be the new kid on the block. The goal with this "style" is to open up gin to experimentation, and have the juniper take a back seat. Many lead with strong citrus or floral notes, though not much is off limits. Cucumber, tomato, and even a pungent coffee note might be the forward flavor, while the botanical blend plays second fiddle.

Plymouth: Plymouth gin as a brand predates Plymouth gin as a style. (The company still exists and still makes gin.) You'll find it is less juniper-forward than London Dry, and is more earthy. In fact many London Dry gins use the same botanicals as Plymouth, which uses seven; they're just used in different quantities. These botanicals are juniper berry, coriander seed, orange peel, lemon peel, angelica root, green cardamom, and orris root. The two citrus peels and two roots are used in much higher quantities in Plymouth though, and thus the botanical balance is altered dramatically. Some "navy-strength gins," which are really just any gin bottled at 57.1 percent ABV or more, draw on this citrusy and earthy botanical balance to help counteract some of the ethanol burn in the higher proof—including a navy-strength gin from the Plymouth distillery themselves.

COMMON GIN BOTANICALS

You'll come across numerous other botanicals that can go in gin, but the list that follows includes all the classics. They are great ones to keep around as you experiment and come up with your own botanical blend.

For a starting point in the following recipes in this chapter, there's a handy chart with some suggested botanical recipes for your gin on page 132. As you get more familiar, you might challenge the max usage on the chart, as there's a bit of a buffer built into some of my recommendations.

▶ Juniper Berries: a general requirement for gin. Adds a piney, resiny, and herbal aroma and flavor.

▶ Orange Peel: both bitter orange peel and sweet orange peel can be used. A classic citrus note in many gins.

▶ Lemon Peel: a much brighter citrus note than orange, it can quickly unbalance other botanicals, but also adds a refreshing and pleasant aroma and flavor.

▶ Coriander Seed: in almost as many gins as juniper, coriander seed adds both a fruity spice flavor as well as a subtle nuttiness.

▶ Orris Root: the root of an iris, it's earthy, floral, and grassy. A complex base note that really brings flavors together in gin quite well.

▶ Licorice Root: (or liquorice) a traditional sweetener that still turns up in a large number of gins. A slight anise spice to the flavor.

▶ Angelica Root: bitter and herbaceous, it plays against citrus notes and sits next to juniper well, accentuating some of the herbal character of each.

▶ Cassia/Cinnamon Bark: the two are quite similar, to the point you might be buying one or the other and not know it. A classic and pungent, earthy spice.

▶ Almonds: both sweet and bitter almond is used in gin. Almond can add a nutty aroma and a marzipan-like flavor.

▶ Nutmeg: a sweet spiciness that seems to be gaining some favor in gin for its pleasant aroma and slightly sweet finish it may add.

▶ Ginger: a peppery, hot, spicy aroma makes this a fun choice to add a recognizable spice note to a gin.

▶ Cardamom: a certain fruity and floral character that is both refreshing and potentially overpowering if used in too large a quantity.

▶ Peppercorn: black or pink, it could be any type of peppercorn. A tart spiciness that can come across as almost fruity.

▶ Cubeb Berries: somewhat like pepper, but more dynamic, with lemon and pine notes, and a bit of floral aroma that comes through.

▶ Grains of Paradise: a sharp pepperiness that's a real palate cleanser if used in larger quantities.

▶ Star Anise: often described as having a pleasant sweetness, not overbearing, and with a nice, exotic, spicy aroma that can sit back or be the star.

▶ Fennel Seed: when you're looking for some spice but don't want to overdo it, fennel can be substituted for other more strongly spicy items like anise, grains of paradise, or pepper.

GIN BOTANICAL BLENDS CHART (FOR A 5-GALLON WASH FROM 12 TO 15 PERCENT ABV)					
BOTANICAL	RECOMMENDED MAX USAGE (60 G TOTAL IN COMBINATION)	LONDON DRY	OLD TOM	NEW AMERICAN	PLYMOUTH
Juniper	45 g	30 g	15 g	12 g	25 g
Orange Peel	6 g		4 g (sweet)	6 g (bitter)	5 g (sweet)
Lemon Peel	6 g	4 g			3 g
Coriander Seed	15 g	8 g	4 g	10 g	10 g
Orris Root	4 g	2 g		3 g	2 g
Licorice Root	8 g	2 g	8 g		
Angelica Root	4 g	3 g			4 g
Cassia/Cinnamon Bark	5 g	3 g	2 g		
Almonds	15 g	5 g (bitter)			
Nutmeg	3 g			1 g	
Ginger	3 g		1 g		
Cardamom	1 g			0.25 g	0.5 g
Peppercorn	6 g		1 g (black)	2 g (pink)	
Cubeb Berries	6 g	1 g		2 g	
Grains of Paradise	4 g	0.5 g			
Star Anise	4 g		1 g		
Fennel Seed				1 g	

Note: This chart will safely guide you through your first experiments with botanicals. The recommended max usage of each botanical is provided as a guardrail; you may find you prefer more. You may want to highlight one of the botanicals, in which case more will be needed. There are many other botanicals besides these you'll want to explore. Different fruit peels and other exotic spices will surely lend a personal touch to your gin.

MACERATION INFUSION FOR GIN OR SCHNAPPS

Take comfort in this: There is no wrong way to infuse flavor into a neutral spirit to make gin or schnapps. Maceration simply means that you'll be soaking your chosen infusion for 24–48 hours in your stripping run spirit or in your neutral spirit following distillation to get the flavor and aroma (the latter will possibly color). Think about what you're adding: If it's dried or dehydrated, you'll want to make sure that the flavor inside is accessible through dissolution—that alcohol can soak it well enough to pull the flavors out. For example, something like whole nutmeg or a dry vanilla bean may need to be opened to get the best results in your spirit. Take a mortar and pestle to crush your botanicals and release the oil and acids inside.

With something like lemon, a classic fruit that's often steeped to make limoncello, all you need to do is cut it up, peel and all, and the juice and liquid will easily seep out and into the alcohol via osmosis. Using a neutral spirit at the highest alcohol possible does help make the infusion process easier on the fruits and herbs, as ethanol is lighter than water and can easily seep into fruits and herbs and pull out flavor and aroma. Of course, shaking, muddling, and mashing along the way is never a bad idea. Use a muslin bag or cheesecloth for any large chunks. Also remember you can filter through a muslin bag, coffee filter, or even a charcoal filter when maceration is complete.

SCHNAPPS

Rounding out the neutral spirits in this chapter, schnapps can be made from just about any neutral spirit that has been infused postdistillation (and generally sweetened as well). In short, vodka is usually consumed as a neutral spirit, gin is infused with botanicals during distillation, and schnapps is infused with any variety of things postdistillation.

Schnapps follows a similar history as vodka and gin. It was infused initially for medicinal purposes, and the tradition of fermenting fruit and infusing it postdistillation continued into our modern day. In a global context, schnapps can be quite different from country to country. In many parts of the world, schnapps can be made from any base sugar, just like gin and vodka. However, in Austria, Hungary, and Switzerland it's often a brandy, which is any spirit distilled from fruit, yet the term schnapps is still used. (Take a look at the brandy recipes in Chapter 8 for more on this type of "schnapps.")

This might sound like an infused vodka, yet if you try commercial examples, you will notice a difference. Infused schnapps is generally much stronger in flavor and sweeter than flavored vodkas, whereas vodkas tend to not have very strong flavors added to them, or sugar for that matter (though that has changed in recent years). Schnapps may have an herbal blend or fruit infused in it for quite some time postdistillation, and it may take on the color and character of those herbs and fruit(s) as well. Whole or larger segmented botanicals, herbs, spices, vegetables, or fruits are used in larger glass or ceramic jugs. As I mentioned, schnapps is often sweeter, with any variety of sugar being added postdistillation as well. If it's heavily sweetened or has some sort of cream added to it for sweetness, and the alcohol is 30 percent or lower, then it most likely crosses over and is considered a liqueur.

EASY NEUTRAL SPIRIT (FOR VODKA, GIN, OR SCHNAPPS)

This recipe and the one on page 139 are quite different, but both will work for vodka, gin, or schnapps. The difference comes through in their taste and is easily noticed if you make both and sample side by side. This recipe is meant to be as clean and neutral as possible.

Note: **Most countries consider a neutral spirit to be between 90 to 95 percent ABV and may even stipulate that vodka needs to reach this high rectification before being diluted to 40 percent ABV to be called vodka. This is often why vodka is double or triple distilled, to reach this high ABV.**

- Makes around 5 gallons (19 liters) of wash
- OG: 1.1109–1.1113 | FG: 0.990–0.998 | ABV: 14–15%

MAKE THE WASH

1. Add the 150 g of Distiller's Nutrient Light Spirits to your clean and sanitized fermenter.

2. Fill the fermentation vessel with 3 gallons (11 liters) of water at around 92°F (33°C) and slowly pour and stir in the 15 lb. of dextrose a few pounds at a time.

3. Once the sugar is fully stirred in and dissolved, top up the fermenter with another 2 gallons (8 liters) of room temperature water.

YOU WILL NEED:

- ▶ 5 oz (150 g) Still Spirits Distiller's Nutrient Light Spirits
- ▶ 15 lb. (7 kg) dextrose (corn sugar)
- ▶ 20 g Still Spirits Distiller's Yeast (vodka or gin)
- ▶ Botanicals basket and botanicals (for gin only)

For a complete list of equipment you'll need, please see pages 11–13.

Make sure all equipment and surfaces have been cleaned and sanitized.

4. Add the Distiller's Yeast directly to the liquid, sprinkling over the top.

5. Close your fermenter with a lid or stopper, as well as an airlock, and leave to ferment around 72°F (22°C), being sure to keep it between 67 to 75°F (19 to 24°C) for at least 14 days.

DISTILLING

6. Transfer your wash to your still (ideally a packed column still or other type of reflux still).

7. At this point it's always good to follow the instructions that came with your still, as they should guide you toward producing a neutral spirit, our current goal. More information on distilling can also be found in Chapter 3. Once you are ready to distill, be sure to

   ▸ Discard the first 50 ml out of your still.

   ▸ Begin collecting in bulk, slowly ramping up the temperature on your still.

   ▸ Perform a stripping run, collecting alcohol until your spirit is coming out at around 20 percent ABV.

8. For vodka or schnapps, perform a spirit run. Dilute your spirit to 40 percent when adding it back to the boiler. Collect the first 250 ml as heads. Then collect all further spirit over 90 percent ABV as your hearts. This will be the best option for your vodka. Collect, save, and recycle your heads and tails for your next run. The remaining steps are for gin only.

9. For gin, take your spirit from the stripping run and add to your boiler (unpacked column still or a pot still boiler). Fill a botanicals basket (gin basket) with your botanicals (see suggestions on page 132), or add them directly to the boiler if you don't have a basket. It's best to tightly pack a botanicals basket to force the vapor up through the herbs and spices. If adding directly to the boiler you may want to add more herbs and spices than recommended, one and a half to two times as much, as adding them to the boiler is a less effective method of extracting their flavors and aromas. You may also want to put them in a cotton (muslin) bag; otherwise you should closely monitor the run to be sure the botanicals don't boil up, blocking your vapor and creating pressure.

10. Run your spirit a second time, your botanical infusion run. If for any reason your collected stripping run is over 35 percent ABV, add water to the boiler until you've reached a spirit that is at 35 percent ABV.

11. Run your still on as low a heat or power setting as you can, giving your vapor as much opportunity to pass through your botanicals basket slowly, and so that you can make proper cuts. Follow Chapter 4's instructions for making cuts from your still. Heads and tails can be reused in future stripping gin runs, but you'll want to choose the best cuts that represent your spirit and botanicals and blend these.

12. Cut with clean water to 40 percent ABV (80 proof), and bottle (see Chapter 6 for tips on bottling).

SCHNAPPS

If you ran the still to make vodka, you can easily turn this into schnapps with a fruit infusion. Remove any hard seeds or pits, as well as stems. Top up a jar with cut fruit and pour the uncut, full-strength neutral spirit over the fruit until the jar is full. Let this sit for at least three weeks, and up to three months, at room temperature. Strain the fruit out using a muslin bag or coffee filter. Cut to 30 percent ABV or to your preference between 20 percent and 40 percent ABV. Add sugar until the sweetness complements the fruit and alcohol.

USING SPIRIT FLAVORINGS AND ESSENCES

There are a variety of companies that make essences or flavorings to emulate your favorite spirits, and you may even be able to try and clone your favorite commercial examples. Some of these products can be quite good and at the least can make a great way to diversify a liquor cabinet once you have a lot of neutral spirit. Read reviews online and then give one a try!

NEUTRAL WHEAT SPIRIT

Wheat is considered one of the best bases for vodka, and in the Eastern European countries, such as Poland and Belarus, where vodka is popular, wheat is the primary source of sugar. While this wheat-based recipe is modeled on a traditional premium vodka, it is also an excellent base for gin or schnapps. (It could also be made into a nice clean wheat whiskey if it was run through a pot still twice instead of a column, and then aged on oak.) This recipe uses raw wheat as is traditional—it adds just a subtle hint of grassiness to the nose and finishes surprisingly smooth.

▸ Makes around 5 gallons (19 liters) of finished wash

▸ OG: 1.060–1.070 | FG: 0.996–1.004 | ABV: 8.7%

MAKE THE WASH

1. Review the section on cereal mashing on page 28 to be sure you understand the process.

2. Add 3.8 gallons (14 liters) of water to your mash tun or kettle.

3. Stir in 12 g of alpha-amylase enzyme and crushed raw wheat and rice hulls.

4. Slowly bring to a boil, constantly stirring.

5. Hold at a boil for 30 minutes.

6. Cover your kettle or mash tun, holding your temperature above 185°F (85°C) for 60 minutes.

7. Add 1 quart of room temperature water and stir.

YOU WILL NEED:

▸ 12 g alpha-amylase enzyme

▸ 15 lb. (7 kg) raw wheat

▸ 0.75 lb. (340 g) rice hulls

▸ 20 g Still Spirits Distiller's Yeast (vodka or gin)

▸ 12 g glucoamylase enzyme

▸ 4 oz (100 g) Still Spirits Distiller's Nutrient Light Spirits (optional)

▸ Botanicals basket and botanicals (for gin only)

For a complete list of equipment you'll need, please see pages 11–13.

Make sure all equipment and surfaces have been cleaned and sanitized.

8. Allow temperature to drop to 149°F (65°C) and add 12 g of glucoamylase enzyme.

9. Allow temperature to naturally drop to 139°F (59°C) and hold for 60 minutes.

10. Heat 3.8 gallons (14 liters) of sparge water to 180°F (82°C) and sparge grain. Optional: You may choose to bring wort to a boil to ensure wort is free from bacteria (sterile) prior to fermentation, and to condense the wort down. To ensure a sterile wort, 15 minutes is ample time, and up to an hour should condense wort to less than 5 gallons, should space in your fermenter or still be an issue. Neither is required if your equipment is clean and your fermenter is at least 6 gallons, large enough to manage around 5.3 gallons of wort.

12. Cool collected wort (it should be around 5.3 gallons if you haven't boiled) and add it to your sanitized fermenter.

13. Pitch yeast once the temperature is below 90°F (32°C).

14. Ferment between 68 and 76°F (20 and 24°C) for 14 days. These cooler temperatures near the bottom of the yeast's range improve the chances of a very clean distillate.

DISTILLING

15. Transfer your wash to your still (ideally a packed column still or other type of reflux still).

16. At this point it's a good idea to follow the instructions that came with your still, as they should guide you toward producing a neutral spirit, our current goal. More information on distilling can also be found in Chapter 3. Once you are ready to distill, be sure to

   ▸ Discard the first 50 ml out of your still.

   ▸ Begin collecting in bulk slowly ramping up the temperature on your still.

   ▸ Perform a stripping run, collecting alcohol until your spirit is coming out at around 20 percent ABV.

17. If making vodka, or a neutral base for schnapps, perform a spirit run. Dilute your spirit to 40 percent when adding it back to the boiler. Collect the first 250 ml as heads. Then collect all further spirit over 90 percent ABV as your hearts. This will be the best option for your vodka or schnapps. Collect, save, and recycle your heads and tails for your next run. The remaining steps are for gin only.

18. For gin, take your spirit from the stripping run and add to your boiler (unpacked column still or a pot still boiler). Fill a botanicals basket (gin basket) with your botanicals (see suggestions on page 132) or add them directly to the boiler if you don't have a basket. It's best to tightly pack a botanicals basket to force the vapor up through the herbs and spices. If adding directly to the boiler you may want to add more herbs and spices than recommended, one and a half to two times as much, as adding them to the boiler is a less effective method of extracting their flavors and aromas. You may also want to put them in a cotton (muslin) bag; otherwise you should closely monitor the run to be sure the botanicals don't boil up, blocking your vapor and creating pressure.

19. Run your spirit a second time, your botanical infusion run for your gin. If for any reason your collected stripping run is over 35 percent ABV, add water to the boiler until you've reached a spirit that is at 35 percent ABV.

20. Run your still on as low a heat or power setting as you can, giving your vapor as much opportunity to slowly pass through your botanicals basket, and so that you can make proper cuts. Follow Chapter 4's instructions for making cuts from your still. Heads and tails can be reused in future stripping gin runs, but you'll want to choose the best cuts that represent your spirit and botanicals and blend these.

21. Cut with clean water to 40 percent ABV (80 proof), and bottle (see Chapter 6 for tips on bottling).

RUM AND NEXT-STEP RECIPES
Chapter 8

Once you have a good idea of how the mashing, fermentation, distilling, and aging processes work, and how best to adapt them to your still and setup, you can start playing around with additional recipes and experimenting with your distillation process. The recipes in this chapter provide a few options easy enough for just about any beginning distiller.

Most of this chapter will focus on rum, which is an ideal bridge between clear/neutral spirits and whiskey. However, I am including a couple of bonus recipes for other spirits like brandy and tequila so you can see the similarities and differences as you build your base of knowledge.

RUM

Rum was first made in the 1600s in the Caribbean. Early "rumbullion," shortened in time to "rum," was likely made from sugarcane juice as well as molasses. After all, sugarcane, molasses, and rum all played a major role in the slave trade to the Americas. There was a need for manpower in the Caribbean to produce sugar for North America and Europe, so slave ships headed to the Caribbean, and molasses and rum were soon a source of currency.

Nowadays the critical ingredient to rum is still molasses—it is even a requirement molasses be used in some countries to designate a product as rum. Otherwise, most forms of sugar cane and sugar cane by-product, such as cane juice, raw sugars, treacles, dark cane sugar, brown sugars, and muscovados, are used. Blackstrap molasses is the most popular. Because it's not as useful or popular in foods or cooking, blackstrap is often the cheapest molasses one can buy, and for that reason a large amount of it globally ends up as rum. The fact that it is low grade doesn't mean as a home distiller you should avoid blackstrap.

Molasses is considered a by-product from the sugar refining process. Blackstrap is typically the darkest, from the third and final evaporation and processing, leaving it with the least amount of sugar. However, when it comes to distilling, it comes with other benefits, notably a bit of nutrient for the yeast. It typically contains 50 to 70 percent sugar, but usually falls on the lower end, with other grades of molasses (light, medium, and dark) closer to 70 percent. The flavor molasses imparts is critical to the congener and ester development of rum throughout the fermentation, distilling, and aging process, and to how the final product ultimately tastes. For this reason, blackstrap is desirable, being quite strong in flavor.

There are numerous styles of rum. Here are some of the most popular:

Light Rum: Also referred to as white rum, "light" doesn't just refer to color, but also to ester content and the "heaviness" of flavor inside the rum. Of all the rums, this one often doesn't have quite the same development or depth of flavor, though the sweet smell and flavor of molasses may still be dominant. It's typically polished postdistillation and may actually sit on the charcoal (active carbon) for some time before it is bottled. It may be aged on oak for a short period of time to develop some of the flavors and then polished again to remove the color.

Amber Rum: Sometimes called gold rum, this can be a delicate and mellow rum that often contains a larger amount of sugar cane juice in the recipe. Amber rums are often spiced rums as well.

Dark Rum: Also known as heavy rum (heavy in congeners, esters, and flavor) or black rum, this rum contains all the rich flavors of dark charred barrels, congeners, and esters left in the spirit during aging, all derived from blackstrap molasses. Big flavors of caramel, vanilla, and molasses should come through. Long aging is fairly critical to this style and has gained quite a following with spirit connoisseurs.

Overproof Rum: May be called navy, cask, or barrel-strength rum, this is a true gentleman's sipping rum, with a big ethanol finish. Overproof rum comes in at a minimum of 50 percent ABV (100 proof) and can be upward of 85 percent ABV (170 proof)!

Agricole: Agricole, or rhum, is made strictly from cane juice. When you see the "h" in the word "rhum," you know it's a straight sugar cane juice product. Although this isn't a traditional rum, it's often treated as such in distilleries around the Caribbean. You won't get those molasses flavors but a much more delicate spirit, and it can be both aged and clear.

RON EXTRA AÑEJO

DIPLOMÁTICO

Reserva

RON EXTRA AÑEJO
RARE RUM SELECTION

Producido por / Produced by /
Destilerías Unidas, S.A.
RIF: J-30940783-0

70 cl ℮   Ron / Rum / Rhum   alc. 40% / vol.

GRAND
GOLD
QUALITY
AWARD
2009

SINCE 1961

Spiced Rum: Infused with a spice blend, spiced rums feature these classic spices: vanilla, orange peel, nutmeg, cinnamon, star anise, cardamom, cloves, allspice, and peppercorn. Popular first with amber rums, there's been a movement for big spice flavors in dark rums as well. Set aside some rum for experimentation; spiced rum can be really fun.

Flavored Rum: These rums have had fruit or other flavorings infused or macerated in. Common flavors are vanilla, honey, coconut, lime, and orange, but more tropical and local fruits show up in rum across the Caribbean and Americas. Flavored rums usually start with clear rum, and in some instances the flavoring (say a vanilla bean or fruit) lives on in the bottle when it goes to retail and at some point, to your home. Why not get the most flavor out of that infusion that you can?

I think you'll find rum is a great spirit that's not hard to make. It starts with sugars that are readily available, and it can be left to age, or not. It can be infused or flavored, single or double distilled, made on a pot or column still (though this does have a significant effect on the flavor), and aged in new or used oak or wood of almost any type. It loves to be blended with other types of rum to create entirely new products. It's unique and flavorful in almost any form—perfect in mixed drinks, over ice, or neat.

EASY DARK RUM

This first recipe can be used to make almost any type of rum. It uses black-strap molasses exclusively as the sugar along with yeast and some nutrients— just to make sure the yeast has all the vitamins and minerals it needs to make it through fermentation completely (though as discussed there are some nutrients in molasses as well). You might find this recipe is all you need to fill a barrel, and a liquor cabinet, with a variety of rums!

▸ Makes around 5 gallons (19 liters) of wash

▸ OG: 1.088–1.100 | FG: 1.000–1010 | ABV: 10.5–12%

MAKE THE WASH

1. Add 50 g of Distiller's Nutrient Dark Spirits to your empty fermenter. Be sure it's a minimum 6-gallon (23-liter) capacity as fermentation may be quite active and will need room to work.

2. Fill the fermentation vessel with 3 gallons (11 liters) of water at around 90°F (32°C) and slowly pour and stir in 20 lb. (9 kg) blackstrap molasses.

3. Once the molasses is fully dissolved, top up the fermenter with about 2 gallons (8 liters), or up to 5.25 gallons (20 liters) in your fermenter. You can use room temperature or warm water at around 90°F (32°C).

4. Add the rum Distiller's Yeast directly to the liquid, sprinkling over the top.

5. Close your fermenter with a lid or stopper and airlock and leave to ferment between 75 and 92°F (24 and 33°C) for 2 weeks. Warm temperatures are great for dark rums, as it helps develop the robust congeners and esters that are traditional.

YOU WILL NEED:

▸ 2 oz (50 g) Still Spirits Distiller's Nutrient Dark Spirits

▸ 20 lb. (9 kg) blackstrap molasses

▸ 20 g Still Spirits Distiller's Yeast (rum)

▸ 1.5- to 2-gallon (6- to 8-liter) medium toast oak barrel, new or used for rum (or 60 g medium toast oak chips)

For a complete list of equipment you'll need, please see pages 11–13.

Make sure all equipment and surfaces have been cleaned and sanitized.

DISTILLING

6. Transfer your molasses wash to your still and follow the cuts for a single run as recommended on page 65.

7. Taste your cuts of heads, hearts, and tails to get familiar with their flavors. Use just your hearts, and possibly some small portions of your heads and tails if these taste adequate to you. Try to aim for a spirit around 70 percent ABV (140 proof) for aging and blend your cuts into a barrel or over oak chips. Optional: Cool the remaining liquid left in the still and use this dunder (or stillage) in your next wash. Use up to 1 gallon (4 liters) or no more than 20 percent of your total volume in your next wash, adding directly to the fermenter.

AGING

The goal is to age for a minimum of 3 months and if possible, for at least 1 year.

For clear rum, you may want to try a double distillation and not finishing the rum on oak. Or maybe polish a portion or all of the spirit after 3 months of aging.

For amber rum, consider aging for 3 weeks on 30 g of oak. If you'd like a bit more color and flavor, leave it another week.

For a spiced rum, you have two options:

1. In a muslin bag or directly in the distilled (possibly aged) spirit, add the following: 2 whole allspice berries, 2 whole cloves, 1 segment of a star anise pod, ½ cinnamon stick, 1 whole cardamom pod, half a vanilla bean split open, and 1" by 1" (2.5 cm by 2.5 cm) square of orange peel with the white pith removed. Steep for 2 weeks. Taste and adjust as needed by adding more or different spices. To sweeten, add a tablespoon at a time of dark brown sugar; mix and taste.

2. Do a double distillation and use a botanicals basket during the second spirit run to infuse the spirit. Fill the basket with the following: 8 allspice berries, 8 cloves, 1 star anise pod, 1 cinnamon stick (chipped into smaller bits is fine), 2 whole cardamom pods, 1 whole vanilla bean split open and segmented into ¼" pieces, and four ½" by ½" (1 cm by 1 cm) squares of orange peel with the white pith removed. Do your spirit run as you would, and either enjoy it clear or age it further.

DISTILLING WITH DUNDER

Dunder, similar to the backset used to make sour mash whiskey, can be the key to fruity, funky, and flavorful rums (like your favorites from the Caribbean). Once you've distilled your first batch of rum, you can start your own "dunder pit," which can simply be a bucket or bin filled with the leftovers in your boiler from a run. You can cover the dunder, but traditionally it's allowed to breathe, taking in the air, including any bacteria and wild yeast present. As it sits, mold may form, bacteria will grow, and wild yeast will settle in to their new home. This mixture of fermenting organisms in the liquid creates a complex cocktail of congeners and esters in the resulting wash. Try adding 5 to 10 percent of your dunder back into your fermentations (¼ to ½ in a 5-gallon wash) to start creating your own unique flavors.

Once you know your dunder quite well, you may want to experiment with more. Traditionally it can be added up to one third of the liquid in a fermenter. Just be cautious as the bacteria and wild yeast can overwhelm your fermentation. Other things, like a pH too low for your yeast to work, or a bacteria content so high that it overwhelms the fresh yeast, can happen.

A wonder, Dunder is a creative tool when making rum. Have some fun with it!

TRADITIONAL WHITE RUM (LIGHT RUM)

White or light rum, sometimes called silver rum, is the perfect cocktail rum to keep around for those less keen to enjoy spirits straight. It is the key to great daiquiris, mojitos, and piña coladas. Be sure to use some sort of yeast nutrients when making this rum, as the little that's in the molasses won't be enough to help the yeast through the more refined brown sugar. This type of rum is not typically aged on oak—yet it is sometimes left to age for quite a while in stainless steel or glass vessels. If you do this, be sure to let a little bit of evaporation and oxygen comingle with the spirit.

- Makes around 5 gallons (19 liters) of wash
- OG: 1.094 | FG: 1.023 | ABV: 9.4%

MAKE THE WASH

1. Add 50 g of Distiller's Nutrient Light Spirits to your empty fermenter.

2. Fill the fermentation vessel with 3 gallons of water at around 92°F (33°C) and slowly pour and stir in the 8 lb. (4 kg) of molasses and 4 lb. (2 kg) of brown sugar.

3. Once the sugars are fully dissolved, top up the fermenter with another 2 gallons of room temperature water, until you have 5.25 gallons (20 liters) total.

YOU WILL NEED:

- 50 g Still Spirits Distiller's Nutrient Light Spirits
- 8 lb. (4 kg) molasses
- 4 lb. (2 kg) light brown sugar
- 20 g Still Spirits Distiller's Yeast (rum)
- 1.5–2-gallon (6–8 liter) medium toast oak barrel, new or used for rum (or 100 g medium toast oak chips)

For a complete list of equipment you'll need, please see pages 11–13.

Make sure all equipment and surfaces have been cleaned and sanitized.

4. Add the rum Distiller's Yeast directly to the liquid, sprinkling over the top.

5. Close the fermenter with a lid or stopper, as well as an airlock, and leave to ferment between 69 and 80°F (21 and 27°C) for around two weeks. Fermentation temperatures toward 80 are okay, but in a clear rum, keeping your fermentation cooler will limit the more dramatic molasses/estery flavors, which is probably preferable.

DISTILLING

6. ransfer your wash to your still. A pot still will give you the most flavor and a packed reflux will provide the least amount of flavor. Follow the process for a double distillation on page 67, making cuts and separating heads, hearts, and tails.

7. Taste your cuts of heads, hearts, and tails to get familiar with their flavors. Take just your hearts, and possibly some small portions of your heads and tails, as you so choose. Try to aim for a spirit around 70 percent ABV (140 proof). Optional: Cool the remaining liquid left in the still and use this "dunder" (or stillage) in your next wash. Use up to 1 gallon (4 liters) or no more than 20 percent of your total volume in your next wash, especially one for a dark rum, adding directly to the fermenter as part of your liquid.

AGING

You may choose to age your rum for up to a year without oak (using glass or stainless steel). Prior to bottling (see Chapter 6), polish the spirit, some or all of it, depending on your preference. If you find the current flavor too "strong," or feel there's an aroma or flavor that is off-putting in the spirit, you'll have to make tougher blending decisions. Clear rum should still retain some molasses sweetness but should otherwise be quite clean in flavor. Cut to 40 percent ABV (80 proof) and enjoy!

YEAST—JUST PITCH MORE!

Haven't seen fermentation kick off yet? Go through this checklist:

▸ **Did you pitch in the yeast? You can always pitch more!**

▸ **Did you kill your yeast, pitching it into your wort while it was still too hot (104°F or higher)? You can always pitch more!**

▸ **Was your yeast expired? You can always pitch in more!**

But before you do all this, is the temperature too low for the yeast? Try adjusting to get it into the yeast's optimal range before adding more.

EASY APPLE OR GRAPE BRANDY

Brandy is any distillate made from fruit, using the fruit's naturally occurring sugar for fermentation. It doesn't matter what sort of still you use, or if it's aged or left clear. Store bought apple juice (or cider) and grape juice is a fun and easy way to start making brandy. When fermented, most fruit juice will yield 4 to 5 percent ABV. You won't get as much spirit as you would a higher alcohol wash, but one way around this is to purchase condensed (frozen) apple or grape juice in cans (no additives or preservatives is best) to add an additional sugar boost directly to your juice. You can also add sugar to boost the ABV of your wash (also known as chaptalization), but this will dilute the fruit flavor in the finished product. Stick to full fruit and you'll be making calvados and cognac (apple and grape brandy, respectively, from France) in no time.

▸ Makes about 5 gallons (19 liters) of wash

▸ OG: 1.040–1.060 | FG: 0.990–0.992 | ABV: 5–8%

YOU WILL NEED:

▸ 5 gallons (19 liters) 100% apple juice or 100% grape juice

▸ 5 tsp Fermax Yeast Nutrient (optional)

▸ 5 g Lalvin EC-1118 yeast

▸ 60 g light to medium char oak chips or barrel (optional)

For a complete list of equipment you'll need, please see pages 11–13.

Make sure all equipment and surfaces have been cleaned and sanitized.

MAKE THE WASH

1. Add 5 gallons of room temperature juice into your empty fermenter. If using, stir in the 5 tsp of yeast nutrient.

2. Sprinkle the Lalvin EC-1118 yeast over the juice.

3. Close your fermenter with a lid or stopper and airlock. Let it ferment between 72 and 84°F (22 and 29°C) for 14 days.

DISTILLING AND AGING

4. Follow the instructions that came with your still, as they should guide you toward producing a neutral spirit, our current goal. More information on distilling can also be found in Chapter 3. Once you are ready to distill, be sure to

   ▸ Discard the first 50 ml out of your still.

   ▸ Begin collecting in bulk, slowly ramping up the temperature on your still.

   ▸ Transfer your wash to the still and follow instructions for a double distillation as found on page 67

5. Be sure when blending cuts to keep spirit with some of the fruit aroma as it's critical to the drinker to understand and appreciate the fruit in the brandy. Optional: Age on medium char oak for a minimum of 3 weeks and up to 2 years.

6. Take the portion of your spirit run you've decided to keep and cut to 40 percent ABV with clean water. Bottle (see Chapter 6 for tips on bottling) and enjoy!

IDEAS FOR BRANDY

Consider purchasing a wine kit from your local home brew shop to make into a brandy. You can also use commercial wine and cut the fermentation process out completely! Note you can add sugar to sweeten your brandy, or you can try adding juice or juice concentrate in small quantities to sweeten and flavor your brandy as well. Add chopped apples, grape, or other fruit directly to your maturing brandy for even more flavor development.

REGIONAL BRANDIES MADE FROM FERMENTED FRUIT		
FRUIT	REGION	TYPE OF BRANDY
Cherry	Switzerland	Kirsch
Apricot, pear, plum, cherry	Hungary	Pálinka
Grape	Chile	Pisco
Plum, grape, sour cherries	Eastern Europe	Rakia (Rakija)
Plum	Central and Eastern Europe	Slivovitz
Plum	Romania	Tuica

EASY BLANCO TEQUILA

If you can source blue agave syrup, tequila is an easy, fun, and rewarding spirit to distill. The beginning—the harvesting and processing of the blue agave—is actually the toughest part of the entire process, as the heart of the plant can weigh up to 200 pounds. Luckily, that's not something you'll have to do yourself if you can find the syrup!

Blanco tequila is popular in margaritas, on the rocks, or simply as a shot. Aging tequila can change the character greatly, and aging is done for varying amounts of time. Whether you've decided to bottle your tequila clear, or age it on oak, tequila isn't difficult to produce once you've sourced the blue agave syrup, and with the easy recipe below you'll have a product you'll be happy with.

▸ Makes about 5 gallons (19 liters) of wash

▸ OG: 1.106–1.110 | FG: 0.990–0.992 | ABV: 15–16%

MAKE THE WASH

1. Add 3 gallons (4 liters) of room temperature water into your empty fermenter.

2. Stir in 15 lb. of blue agave syrup until thoroughly mixed. Top up fermenter to 5 gallons total. If using, stir in the 5 tsp of Fermax Yeast Nutrient.

3. Sprinkle the Lalvin QA 23 over the blue agave wash.

4. Close your fermenter with a lid or stopper and airlock. Let it ferment between 75 and 85°F (24 and 29°C) for 14 days.

YOU WILL NEED:

▸ 15 lb. (7 kg) blue agave syrup

▸ 5 tsp Fermax Yeast Nutrient (optional)

▸ 5 g Lalvin QA 23 yeast

▸ 2 oz (60 g) light to medium char oak chips or barrel (optional)

For a complete list of equipment you'll need, please see pages 11–13.

Make sure all equipment and surfaces have been cleaned and sanitized.

DISTILLING AND AGING

5. Follow the instructions that came with your still, as they should guide you toward producing a neutral spirit, our current goal. More information on distilling can also be found in Chapter 3. Once you are ready to distill, be sure to

▸ Discard the first 50 ml out of your still.

▸ Begin collecting in bulk, slowly ramping up the temperature on your still.

▸ Transfer your wash to the still and follow instructions for a double distillation as found on page 67.

TEQUILA DESIGNATIONS

BLANCO: Unaged tequila

REPOSADO: Aged on oak for two to twelve months

ANEJO: Aged one to three years on oak

EXTRA ANEJO: Aged more than three years on oak

JOVEN: A blend of blanco and reposado

Optional: Age on medium char oak for 2 to 12 months make a reposado tequila.

6. Take the portion of your spirit run you've decided to keep and cut it to 40 percent ABV with clean water. Bottle (see Chapter 6 for tips on bottling) and enjoy!

WHISKEY AND WHISKEY RECIPES

Chapter 9

Whiskey, and its assorted variations from bourbon to Scotch, is the holy grail for some distillers. Perhaps no spirit, start to finish, requires such control and experience. From mastering fermentation and distilling to the nuances of tasting and blending spirits aged in wood, it combines art and science in a satisfying way.

Due to this complexity and the extra steps involved (and judgment needed!) when making these spirits, I do recommend starting off with recipes in other chapters, notably neutral spirits, before setting your sights on your first whiskey. Nevertheless, feel free to browse this chapter at any time and compare the recipes to the neutral spirits to see what is the same and what's different.

829

Williams

ORE
1829

KEY
LED

IN IRELAND
OT STILL AND MALT

JACK DANIEL'S

Old
No.7

Old
No.7
BRAND

EVERY DROP MADE IN LYNCHBURG TENNESSEE

Tennessee
SOUR MASH

WHISKEY

70cl 40% Vol.

DISTILLED AND BOTTLED BY
JACK DANIEL DISTILLERY
LYNCHBURG, TENNESSEE 37352 U.S.A.

JIM BEAM

THE WORLD'S No.1 BOURBON

JIM BEAM

JIM BEAM
B
SINCE 1795

TM

BOURBON

KENTUCKY STRAIGHT
BOURBON WHISKEY

James B. Beam

NONE GENUINE WITHOUT MY SIGNATURE

DISTILLED BY
JAMES B. BEAM DISTILLING CO.
BEAM • CLERMONT
FRANKFORT, KENTUCKY USA

40% vol

"Afore ye g

FINE   AGED

BELL'S

LENDED SCOTCH WHISKY

COMMITTED
TO THE SAME
EXACTING

ESTD   1825

Arthur Bell & Sons

PRODUCT OF SCOTLA

ORIGINA

WHISKEY BASICS

Historically, whiskey has been whiskey as we know it now since at least 1608 when Old Bushmills Distillery was licensed in Northern Ireland. Prior to that it had been made in monasteries and farms across much of Europe for at least a century. However, there was no set of rules or laws to define whiskey. Most whiskey may have ended up in wooden casks but not intentionally aged. As is the case with many spirits, taxation played a big role in what whiskey has become.

Whiskey or "whisky," as is proper in Scotland, Canada, Japan, and many other places, is truly a wide-ranging spirit but can be defined by its use of grain and aging on oak. It is more closely defined by local laws by country, which may call for certain grains to be used, certain processes to be followed, and a certain number of years it must be aged. Generally, though, there are two broad categories of whiskey:

1. Malt Whiskey: made mostly (at least 51 percent) or entirely from "malt," or malted barley

2. Grain Whiskey: made mostly (at least 51 percent) or entirely with grains other than malted barley

From there the definitions get a bit more region specific and somewhat convoluted. The major points for defining whiskey are

- What country, state, or region it was made in
- What specific grains were used
- If any nongrains were used
- What strength the whiskey was distilled at
- How long it was aged
- What it was aged in
- If it was blended with any other spirit and where that spirit was made; and
- What strength it was bottled at.

Other processes such as filtering, caramel coloring, flavoring additions, and whether smoked malt (such as peated, or peat-smoked barley, which is used in Scottish whiskys) all have an effect on what a whiskey can and should be called. Consider these examples and their major defining characteristics:

Barrel Proof Whiskey: also known as cask strength, from a single barrel and often times bottled without dilution.

Blended Whiskey: a mixture of different types of whiskey, sometimes from different distilleries. This allows a brand, label, or distillery to keep a very consistent product.

Bourbon: must be aged in new oak barrels and made with at least 51 percent corn.

Canadian Whisky: must be made only from grain and aged in barrels smaller than 185 gallons (700 liters) for at least three years.

Corn Whiskey: from the United States, must contain 80 percent corn, and not be aged (or if aged, done in uncharred or used barrels).

Irish Whiskey: must be made in Ireland and aged in wooden barrels for at least three years.

Rye Whiskey: made from at least 51 percent rye.

Scotch Whisky: must be distilled in Scotland and matured in oak barrels for at least three years.

Straight Whiskey: must be made from only grain and during distillation not be concentrated over 80 percent ABV. It then must be aged in new charred oak barrels for at least two years, at no higher than 125 proof (62.5 percent ABV).

Wheat Whiskey: made from at least 51 percent wheat.

Whiskey is a popular spirit the world over; on par with wine, it varies in age, price, and quality, and it is marketed and premiumized quite well too. Also much like wine, sometimes age, affordability, and accessibility are not always the best ways to judge a good bottle of whiskey. Scotland, Ireland, Canada, the United States, and Japan are some of the largest producers of whiskey in the world, but many other countries are emerging as whiskey producers to help quench their local populations appetite. Australia, Germany, and the United Kingdom all have whiskey distilleries popping up each year. In some of these countries, whiskey has few parameters to follow and is a bit like the Wild West. In India, molasses, a sugar by-product more associated with rum, is often blended in or used as the majority of the sugar base.

MOONSHINE'S MYSTIQUE

Moonshining, the making of illegal spirits, may be associated with the United States and hillbillies all through the Appalachian Mountains, but it actually got its start in Scotland. The English Malt Tax of 1725 meant a significant change in the price of whiskey, one most distillers and their customers couldn't easily afford. This meant a rise in both home distilling and distilling by night for both legal and illegal commercial operations. No better time to distill than by moonlight if you don't want to get caught! And so the name "moonshine" came to be. Sixty-six years later, in 1791, the Whiskey Rebellion, which included the tarring and feathering of at least one tax collector, was sparked by a tax increase in the United States.

Moonshine is now associated with any illegally made spirit, but mostly clear unaged whiskey known by a number of names: white lightning, firewater, mountain dew, and hooch, to name a few. Any of the whiskey recipes in this book can serve as a moonshine recipe, but most distillers use something akin to a bourbon recipe, with plenty of corn and a small amount of malted barley. Others looking to avoid mashing may decrease the amount of malt to nothing, steep or boil a little cracked corn for flavor, and simply ferment dextrose (corn sugar) for their wash.

There are a bunch of ways to make whiskey. As you build your collection of aging whiskeys, you'll be able to make even more different types of blended whiskeys. Your drinking preferences may play a role in what you decide to make. Rye whiskey and peated (smoked) whiskeys have strong flavors that are not everyone's couple of tea... or should I say, dram of whiskey. Also, don't be intimidated by the long aging thinking you can't make great whiskey in a shorter period of time. The quantity of oak you use will have a direct effect on how much character you can add in a few short months, as aging on oak begins to offer smaller, diminishing returns as time goes by.

The "Easy" Malt Whiskey recipe on page 166 is a great first whiskey as it uses liquid malt extract (LME), which is barley malt that has already been mashed. LME makes a good whiskey base sugar with no mashing of grains required! This recipe also provides optional use of grain you can steep that will provide additional caramel, toffee, and other flavors and aromas as the whiskey ages. You may find similar LME from other malting companies that can be substituted. This recipe also uses just one run on your still, requiring you to collect only the best alcohol for the best opportunity for a top-quality whiskey on your first run. I've also detailed the process and what sort of equipment and ingredients in more specifics than you might find in a typical spirits recipe.

WHISKEY OR WHISKY?

In Scotland and Japan it is common to drop the "e" from whiskey when referring to their own whiskeys. Japan's whisky culture is based on that of Scotland's, originating from Japanese chemist and businessman Masataka Taketsuru traveling to Scotland to apprentice in distilleries in 1918. He returned to Japan in 1923 where he laid the foundation for Japan's whisky industry. Scotland's whisky culture had a global influence on most countries producing whiskey, with the United States and Ireland being two of the only countries to adopt spelling whiskey with an "e." Besides the difference in spelling, there's no real distinction between whiskey and whisky; they are one-and-the-same kindred spirits.

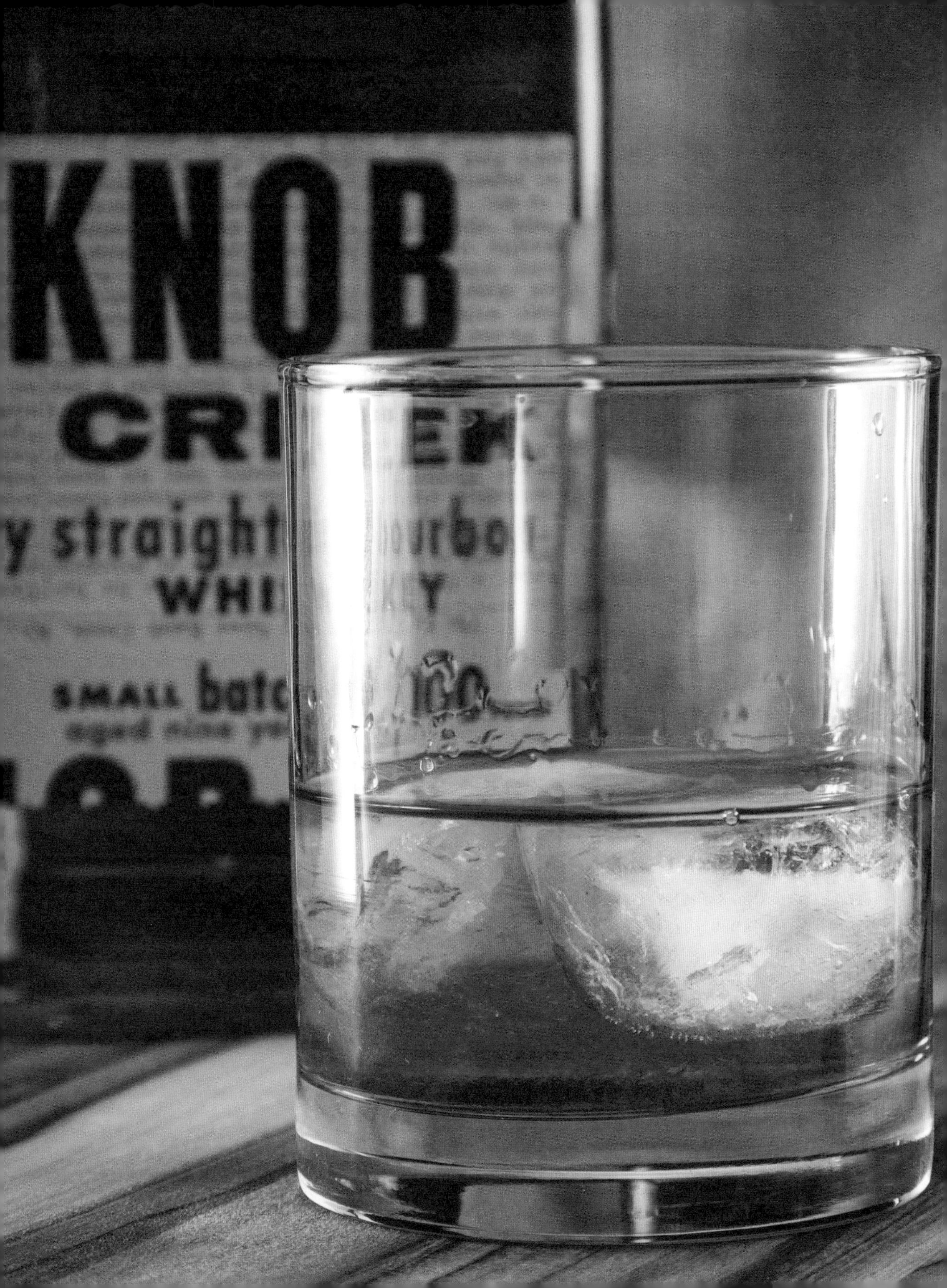
KNOB
SMALL

"EASY" MALT WHISKEY

If you want to get started making whiskey, this is the recipe for you. That said, it is still considerably more complex than most of the recipes in Chapter 7. I recommend starting with a simpler spirit and getting a batch under your belt before tackling even this easy/beginner-level whiskey.

- ▸ Makes 5 gallons (19 liters) of wash
- ▸ OG: 1.086–1.096 | FG: 1.009–1.018 | ABV: 10.6–11.5%

MAKE THE WASH

1. Fill the fermenter with 5 gallons (19 liters) of clean, potable water, which can be warm but not above 90°F (32°C).

2. Slowly stir in the liquid malt extract with your spoon. Be sure the malt extract completely dissolves. If your malt canisters are cold, you may warm them by submerging them in a pot of water on low heat on the stove. After the canisters warm up (around 10 minutes), the malt should pour quite easily from the canister. Use your spoon to scrape out the inside of the canisters, or you may use some of your fermenter's water to rinse the extract from the inside of the canisters.

YOU WILL NEED:

- ▸ 13.2 lb. (6 kg or 4 canisters) Briess CBW Golden Light Liquid Malt Extract, or similar unhopped liquid malt extract
- ▸ 1 lb. (450 g) Simpsons Medium Crystal Malt 60L (optional)
- ▸ 0.5 lb. (225 g) Dingemans Chocolate Malt (optional)
- ▸ 20 g Still Spirits Distiller's Whiskey Yeast
- ▸ 2 oz (60 g) medium toast oak chips

For a complete list of equipment you'll need, please see pages 11–13.

Make sure all equipment and surfaces have been cleaned and sanitized.

Note: Liquid malt extract, or LME, is a popular ingredient in home brewing and can be found online or in most home brew shops. Malt extract is most often made with malted barley on large brewing systems and is mashed and sparged (or lautered—the grains are rinsed of their sugar), just as you would if you were mashing to make a wash. The difference is that the liquid wort is then sent through an evaporator until it's a syrup and most of the water has been taken out. Dry malt extract (DME) can also be used. If you plan to use DME, it's 20 percent more efficient (no water weight) so cut your usage to 80 percent of LME in a recipe. You will find similar options, though potentially different brands, at your local home brew shop.

3. Take a gravity reading with your hydrometer. You can do this with a wine thief or by filling a sample test jar. Or you can float your hydrometer right in your fermentation vessel. Read the hydrometer's specific gravity at the surface. This reading should be between 1.086 and 1.096. This range takes into account the number of factors that will affect your gravity: how well you cleaned out your extract canisters, how much water you used, and if you decided to steep some grain. If your reading is a bit lower, you may have added a bit more water than 5 gallons; if it's higher, probably a bit less than 5 gallons. That's okay; you may just get slightly more or less wash to run! If you've landed between 1.086 and 1.096, you're in the right range, and on your way to making whiskey!

Optional: For more flavor and aroma development in your final whiskey, you may add 1lb (450 g) Simpsons Medium Crystal Malt 60L and 0.5 lb. (225 g) Chocolate Malt to a muslin or nylon steeping bag, tie the bag off, and sink and stir the crushed grains in your fermenter until the bag and grains are well soaked and have begun to dissolve into the unfermented wort, around 30 seconds. Leave the bag in the fermenter.

4. Sprinkle the entire package of yeast over the top of the unfermented wort. The yeast will rehydrate and begin working in 24 to 48 hours. Keep the yeast in the temperature range recommended by the manufacturer on the package.

5. Be sure to tighten the lid or stopper on your fermenter and place an airlock with water filled to the "fill" line in the grommet or stopper on top.

6. Let your wort (soon to be wash, once alcohol is produced) ferment for 14 days at 70 to 80°F (21 to 27°C). If you don't see any activity in your airlock after 48 hours, it could be

   ▸ Your lid or stopper wasn't in tight.

   ▸ You forgot to put water in your airlock.

   ▸ Your fermentation area is too cool.

   ▸ Or your yeast was old, or you forgot to sprinkle it in!

If any of these are the case, don't panic—your wash is probably just fine. Distillation is a miracle worker on mistakes; it can eliminate many of them made during fermentation. Fix the situation: Fasten your lid tightly, add water to your airlock, warm your fermenter, or sprinkle some more yeast in.

7. If after 14 days your airlock is still bubbling away, let it sit another 2 to 3 days to let fermentation finish. You want fermentation to completely finish or you'll be losing fermentable sugars behind that won't be made into alcohol and end up in your spirit.

You may need to warm the fermenter a few degrees if it's still fermenting after 14 days. Another way to tell if fermentation is finished, or near finished, is if you've reached a terminal gravity (final gravity) of 1.009. If you don't get quite that low, that's fine. You may pull a sample from your fermenter with a wine thief or siphon. Or, if the top of your fermenter is clear of krausen (foam), you may gently drop your hydrometer in your fermenter to check.

If you haven't seen a bubble for at least 24 hours, you know fermentation is done. No rush—going over 14 days is okay; 21 days, 30 days, 60 days? Yep, you're fine, but you'll want to run that wash at some point! Because many folks wonder how long it can sit, I'll say any wash over 10 percent ABV, a pretty high gravity wash, can sit for 90 days without being moved from the still. Any adverse effects this might have should be minimal on a spirit. If under 10 percent ABV, use that wash in 45 days or so.

8. Now that fermentation is complete, if your fermenting bucket doesn't have a spigot, you'll want to sanitize a racking cane or autosiphon and tubing to transfer your wash to the still, leaving behind the optional grain and all of the dead yeast and trub at the bottom of the fermenter.

BACTERIA AND BACKSET

Bacterias such as *lactobacillus* and *pediococcus*, to name a couple, are everywhere: in the air you breathe, on fruit, on meat, in your fermenter, in your wash. Giving it too much time to grow compounds the problem and spoils foods and beverages. There are also wild yeasts like *brettanomyces* that can do the same. Alcohol is good at staving off bacteria, as very few can actually survive in even a little bit. But lower-ABV beers (less than 6 percent) are considered harder to brew because of the need for perfect sanitation, since bacteria like *lactobacillus* can still tolerate the low pH, low oxygen (yeast use it and fill your fermenter with CO_2), and somewhat alcoholic environment. Wines, on the other hand, are often more than 12 percent ABV and have even less chance of infection. Is fermenting a high ABV wash or wine easier than fermenting and making a standard alcohol beer? Yep, there's less chance of spoilage.

Bacterias and wild yeasts create different kinds of congener alcohols as well as acids during fermentation. In small quantities, this can be good for complex flavor but not great for getting a spirit that still has a high ethanol content. It may also create a funky, possibly overly complex, unpredictable, or even "rough" or harsh flavor and alcohol character if bacteria or wild yeast are used in high concentrations.

There are plenty of opportunities to continue your experimentation into the world of bacteria and wild yeast with backset, the practice of reusing what's left in the boiler postdistillation in future fermentations. This is often left to spontaneously ferment with yeast and bacteria and is then added to a new batch of wort if making sour mash whiskey, or to a molasses wash if making rum, where the backset is then called "dunder," just to keep you on your toes.

DISTILLING

9. For this whiskey we'll distill in a single run. While leaving a good amount of flavor, it still gives you the opportunity to blend in cuts. For your run, use a pot still or unpacked column still.

10. Starting at around 145°F (63°C) head temperature (the reading on the thermometer at the top of your still), you may start seeing alcohol come out. A head temperature thermometer can be helpful with a pot still. Discard the first 50 ml out of the still. These first foreshots potentially contain methyl alcohol (methanol), the unpotable bad stuff.

   If your still has voltage or flame control, once your still reaches 168°F (76°C), turn down the heat so that you're not gaining over a degree Fahrenheit every 2 minutes. "Low and slow" is something you'll hear from distillers time and time again regarding the boiler heat and speed at which you should be collecting the spirit, respectively. It's true: you'll get very clean cuts, without a lot of crossover or "smearing" of flavors and alcohols. Begin collecting your run into 10 numbered and labeled 16 oz (500 ml) glass containers. Have the jars and the room to collect at least 1.25 gallons, just over one fifth of your wash. If you have a parrot you are collecting into, or you want to make heads/hearts/tails cuts with your 8 oz (250 ml) glass test jar, you can make your cuts based on proof (see sidebar on page 171).

USING SPECIALTY MALT

Specialty malt is any malt that adds a significant color or flavor contribution compared to a standard base malt. These might have names like caramel, crystal, chocolate, or brown malt. Most of these will not provide the same amount of starch as a distiller's malt. Smoked malts, like peat malt, are specialty malts that can be used as base malts because many still contain large amounts of starch, or they can be used in smaller amounts to contribute flavor.

The use of specialty malts to add flavor to whiskeys is growing in popularity. With smaller, more experimental craft distilleries popping up, the cost associated with making a unique product is less of a concern than for larger whiskey operations. I encourage you to experiment with your whiskey grains and malts, as there's a world of flavors to try!

MAKING WHISKEY CUTS BY PROOF

The most common way to make cuts is by watching your proof. A parrot will make this easier. Some distillers use their still's head temperature to make cuts. This works great if you know your still and your wash, and what to expect when certain temperatures are reached. Making cuts by proof may still require you to get to know your still, but it is the easier method.

Cuts by proof for whiskey:

FORESHOTS: As you would typically do, you'll want to discard the first 50 ml as these likely contain the most methanol.

HEADS (FIRST PART OF THE RUN): These are also sometimes called the foreshots (the same as that first 50 ml you tossed) in whiskey distilling. If you're using a glass test jar, your cuts will be a bit less precise, but best to take and test 250 ml at a time for a nice average. If you're using a parrot, you'll be continuously running it through your parrot into a collection vessel, moving to the next jar when your spirit average in the parrot passes one of the markers for moving to the next cut. For your heads, this will be once you are collecting an average of alcohol at 80 percent ABV (160 proof). If your still isn't efficient enough to run alcohol off this high, at a minimum the first 250 ml out of the still need to be separated off as heads. Or if your still started running below 80 percent ABV (160 proof), mark this down and consider adjusting your heads cut to include down to 70 percent. This first part of your run will include a number of harsh aromatics and flavored volatiles no matter the proof.

HEARTS (MIDDLE OF THE RUN): Alcohol tested and collected should average 50 to 80 percent ABV (100 to 160 proof) when collected or run through your parrot, cutting to tails when your average in your parrot or test jar drops below this.

TAILS (END OF THE RUN): This third cut is also called feints in whiskey distilling. Alcohol tested and collected should average 20 to 50 percent ABV (40 to 100 proof) when collected or run through your parrot, stopping your run when your average in your parrot or test jar drops below 20 percent ABV (40 proof).

You'll end up with three distinctive sets of grouped and hopefully still ordered jars, with some at the end of each cut not very full. Typically any heads collected above 80 percent wouldn't be blended back into a whiskey for aging, except in certain circumstances or certain types of whiskey. But most tails collected would be fair game if you think they might add something to the aging alcohol.

Your goal will be to collect at least a gallon of spirits from your run in total, all cuts included. Collect around 16 oz (500 ml) in each glass container. Your first three, cuts 1 through 3 (48 oz), will generally be your heads; your next four, 4 through 7 (64 oz), will be hearts; and your last three, 8 through 10 (48 oz), will be tails. If you're still getting alcohol out over 20 percent ABV (40 proof) you can continue to collect tails until your spirit is reading less than 20 percent ABV (40 proof) for future runs.

11. Take your four hearts jars from the middle of your run and smell or a taste them if you like. This should be the good stuff. If there are any concerns, set the problem jar aside to potentially add when you're more comfortable with what you smelled or tasted in comparison to your other jars.

12. Add these four together in a glass jug or container that can be made air tight. Smell and taste your jar 3 (last heads jar) and jar 8 (first tails jar) and decide if you'd like to add some or all of either jar to the same jug. If the smell is super strong from the third jar, like paint thinner or nail polish remover, or wet dog or gym socks from the eighth jar, it's best to hold on to these and run them through your still again at a later date. That said, these jars likely have a different character than your hearts jars; their job is to add character. You may only want to add one third or a half from each jar.

13. Go to jars 2 and 9. Anything you want to use from these? If you use any, blend them in cautiously to your jug. It's not uncommon to not use these. As for your first and last jars, jars 1 and 10, I suggest you don't use their contents.

14. Add 60 g medium toast oak chips either loose or in a muslin or nylon bag (you can add rinsed glass marbles if you need to sink the bag) and shake the jug to soak the chips. Let the jug sit for a minimum of 3 months.

15. You may continue adding spirit to this glass aging container until you've reached a gallon if you're making a feints run (see sidebar on page 174) or another whiskey run that you want blended in.

16. Drink at "cask strength" if you dare, or might I suggest adding spring or distilled water to bring your spirit down to 40 percent ABV (80 proof) when ready to bottle and drink. Doing so gives you more whiskey to bottle, drink, and share! Bottle your whiskey from your jug or larger dilution vessel into glass bottles, first filtering using a funnel with a coffee filter to catch small and large particles from the oak chips.

17. Cork or cap tightly, because spirit likes to evaporate! Cheers to you and your successful batch of whiskey!

FOLLOWING UP WITH
A FEINTS RUN

The heads and tails can be rerun through a still on their own, but from a time and energy perspective, it's sometimes more effective to add them to your next wash, or together from multiple runs, a larger collection of heads and tails you've accumulated over time. Feints may refer to the heads and tails, or just the tails. Running a collection of heads and tails on their own is called a feints run, which still produces a good amount of spirit with big flavors and can be blended into your whiskey (or rum). Your feints run will follow a similar method as already described. You can run the 32 to 96 ounces you have from jars 1 through 3 and 8 through 10 on a smaller still like the Still Spirits Air Still, or you could dilute with water until you're at about half the volume of your boiler. This is to make sure your cuts are steady and consistent with the heat you are applying. Half is an appropriate volume for your boiler; you want your run to still be low and slow, and you don't want the boiler to run dry. No matter what, make sure your heads and tails are diluted to at least 40 percent ABV (I like a maximum of 35 percent ABV myself for feints runs) for your still to run appropriately. Too high an alcohol will boil too fast.

If only running around 90 to 100 ounces total of wash for your feints run, use three jars, taking first 8 ounces (your heads, which will smell like acetone), then 16 ounces (hearts), then 16 ounces (tails). The 16 ounces of hearts should taste and smell clean. If it doesn't, it's best to save your entire run for your next wash. Add it to your whiskey or age it on its own for blending in later. You can still save the heads and tails from this feints run for yet another wash if you like.

Scotch whisky is a nice intermediate style of whiskey to make. It's easy enough, using malted barley, which includes all of the enzymes and nutrients you need to successfully mash and ferment. It's often made with a wash with a potential ABV of 6 to 10 percent, which means a manageable amount of grain for your first whiskey mash.

SCOTCH-STYLE WHISKEY

For many, there's nothing better than a Scotch whisky. It's a refined spirit that shows off the distiller's skill as well as deep experience with blending. As with the previous recipe, my words of wisdom are to start with simpler recipes before jumping in to whiskey. Make sure you understand all the parameters and set yourself up for success.

- Makes around 5 gallons (19 liters) of wash
- OG 1.064–1.072 | FG 1.005–1.009 | ABV 7.5–8.5%

MAKE THE WASH

1. Add 4 gallons of water to your mash tun and heat to 160°F (71°C).

2. Stir in the distilling malt and hold the temperature at 148°F (64°C) for 60 minutes.

3. Heat 3.3 gallons (13 liters) of sparge water in your sparge water heater to 180°F (82°C) and sparge/rinse grain with the sparge water. Optional: You may choose to bring the wort to a boil to ensure it is free from bacteria prior to fermentation and to condense it down (15 minutes is ample time to ensure a sterile wort, and up to an hour should be ample to condense wort to less than 5 gallons, should space in your fermenter or still be an issue). Neither is required if your equipment is clean and your fermenter is at least 6 gallons, large enough to manage around 5.25 gallons (20 liters) of wort.

YOU WILL NEED:

- **12 lb. (5.4 kg) Simpsons Pot Still Malt**
- **20 g Still Spirits Whiskey Yeast**
- **New or used 6- to 8-liter medium toast oak barrel (or 60 g medium toast oak chips)**

For a complete list of equipment you'll need, please see pages 11–13.

Make sure all equipment and surfaces have been cleaned and sanitized.

4. Cool the collected wort with wort chiller or an ice bath, or leave it in the fermenter until the temperature is 95°F (35°C). It should be around 5.25 gallons (20 liters) if you haven't boiled. Add it to your sanitized fermenter.

5. Pitch yeast once the temperature is below 95°F (35°C).

6. Ferment between 70 to 80°F (21 to 27°C) for 14 days. Transfer the wash to your still.

DISTILLING AND AGING

7. Distill using a stripping run in a pot still, removing the first 50 ml (the methylated foreshots) and collecting in bulk until your average collected spirit is 35 percent ABV (70 proof).

8. For your second run, your spirit run, discard the foreshots, anything that comes off before your still head temperature reaches 170°F (77°C), or just discard the first 25 ml.

9. Perform proof cuts (see sidebar Making Whiskey Cuts by Proof on page 171) or collect the first 500 ml—this is generally your heads.

10. With your still running slowly and steadily, raising at most a degree every couple of minutes, collect the next part of your run until your still produces 40 percent ABV spirit, or until your still head temperature reaches 180°F (82°C), whichever comes first. This is your hearts.

11. The rest of your run will be tails. Continue to collect until your alcohol begins to run out at less than 20 percent ABV (40 proof).

12. For a clean Scotch-style whiskey, age just the hearts, and continue to add new hearts from spirit runs to your aging spirit. Or for a more flavorful Scotch whisky, perform a feints run (see sidebar Following Up with a Feints Run on page 174) and add half of the hearts of the run to your collected heads.

13. Add to a barrel or to oak chips for a minimum of 6 months (tradition and law require 3 years, but good luck not drinking it before then!).

Optional: Make it peated. For a peat smoked–style Scotch whiskey, use 7 lb. (3 kg) Simpsons Peated Malt in place of 7 lb. (3 kg) of Simpsons Pot Still Malt. Start here and adjust your peat smoked malt quantity in future batches to your taste. If this is too much, make a straight Scotch whiskey without any peat malt and blend it into the peated batch to reach your desired level of smoke.

AVOID THE BARREL BLUES

If aging your spirit for a long time in a barrel, keep in mind the angel's share (your loss of spirit to wood and evaporation) can be quite aggressive on a small barrel! Keep the barrel moist by laying a damp cloth across it, changing it every so often, to keep the staves from drying out on top, or top up occasionally with more spirit. Don't worry about your damp cloth affecting or reaching your spirits inside, because most barrels are too thick—only the outer part of the wood will be affected.

BOURBON-STYLE WHISKEY

The difficulty in making bourbon is mashing unmalted grain such as corn. Because it doesn't need a cereal mash, pregelatinized corn is a great place to start, but it requires care and attention to the process and effective use of enzymes to be the most useful as a provider of sugar to your wash. Rye malt is easier to manage than rye flakes in your mash, as rye flakes like to gelatinize, resulting in a "stuck sparge" (see sidebar on page 180). The rice hulls are in there to help alleviate this potential headache.

- Makes around 5 gallons (19 liters) of wash
- OG: 1.096–1.104 | FG: 1.000–1.010 | ABV: 12–13%

MAKE THE WASH

1. Add 6 gallons (23 liters) of water to your mash tun and heat to 162°F (72°C).

2. Stir in all grains (and optional hulls) and hold the temperature at 148°F (64°C) for 60 minutes.

3. Let the temperature fall in the mash tun to 139°F (59°C). Stir 12 g glucoamylase into the mash.

4. Keep the mash between 123 and 139°F (51 and 59°C) for 1 hour.

YOU WILL NEED:

- 10 lb. (4.5 kg) Briess Brewers Yellow Corn Flakes
- 6 lb. (2.7 kg) Rahr High DP Distiller's Malt
- 2 lb. (1 kg) Gambrinus Rye Malt
- 12 oz (340 g) rice hulls (optional)
- 12 g Still Spirits Distiller's Glucoamylase Enzyme
- 20 g Still Spirits Whiskey Distiller's Yeast
- 6- to 8-liter medium toast or charred oak barrel, new or used for bourbon (or 100 g medium toast oak chips)

For a complete list of equipment you'll need, please see pages 11–13.

Make sure all equipment and surfaces have been cleaned and sanitized.

5. Heat 2.2 gallons (8 liters) of sparge water to 180°F (82°C) and sparge grain. Optional: You may choose to bring the wort to a boil to ensure it is free from bacteria prior to fermentation and to condense it down (15 minutes is ample time to ensure a sterile wort, and up to an hour should be ample to condense wort to less than 5 gallons, should space in your fermenter or still be an issue). Neither is required if your equipment is clean and your fermenter is at least 6 gallons (23 liters), large enough to manage around 5.25 gallons (20 liters) of wort.

6. Cool the collected wort and add to your fermenter.

7. Pitch yeast once the temperature is below 95°F (35°C).

8. Ferment at 72°F (22°C) for 14 days. Transfer the wash to your still.

DISTILLING AND AGING

9. Distill using a single run in a pot still or unpacked column still, or with 3 or fewer plates in a flute still. Remove the first 50 ml and collect in bulk until your average collected spirit is 35 percent ABV (70 proof.)

10. Take 10 even cuts across your run (four 500 ml heads jars, six 500 ml hearts jars, four 500 ml tails jars) or via proof cuts (see sidebar Making Whiskey Cuts by Proof on page 171).

11. Taste the heads, hearts, and tails to get familiar with their flavors.

12. Take just your hearts, and possibly some small portions of your heads and tails; no more than 12 oz (355 ml) of either is recommended for your first bourbon batch. Try to aim for a collected spirit between 50 and 62 percent ABV (100 and 124 proof) for aging. Add it to a barrel or age on oak chips.

13. Age for a minimum of 6 months and, if possible, up to 2 years to make it "straight" bourbon.

Optional: Make it a wheated bourbon. Adding 2 lb. (1 kg) of either wheat flakes or wheat malt instead of rye will give this the beautiful smooth flavor of wheat in a bourbon. Wheated bourbons may be more popular than you think, turning up in the legendary Pappy Van Winkle and Maker's Mark whiskeys.

WHAT'S A STUCK SPARGE?

A stuck sparge happens when you try to rinse grains and nothing comes out. Proteins in unmalted grains are gelatinous and gooey. Bourbon often uses these grains, so you'll need to be on the lookout for a stuck sparge.

A stuck mash is similar; it typically happens during mashing with a recirculation pump, when your wort doesn't freely flow back through your mash to help hold your grains at temperature. If you're using a mash tun with a pump to recirculate, it could be because your pump or tubing/piping has grain lodged in it, but most likely your false bottom or mash screen is plugged with gelatinized grain. If you have a pump, try to reverse it.

If you're sparging and nothing is flowing through your grain, try stirring your mash grains. It's possible the grain bed compressed when you opened your valve to drain off the wort. Adding more water or adding rice or oat hulls (more if you've added some already) might help as well. Nothing working? If you have a large nylon bag around, hook it around a bucket and dump your mash tun out; clean out your piping, pump, and mash screen; and add the entire nylon bag back to your mash tun if you can. Thin out your mash (add lots of water) and see if you're able to sparge. If worse comes to worst, just drain your mash tun the best you can, and use the wort you can collect and sparge. A stuck sparge is a pain, but don't give up on it until you've identified the problem and have no other options for rinsing the grains of their sugary goodness.

CORN WHISKEY

A good general recipe for a whiskey would be something like the corn whiskey below. Due to the high adjunct ratio (unmalted or flaked grain to malt), you will want to use enzymes to help convert all the starch to sugar, as you would typically get these enzymes from malted grain. Add both alpha-amylase and glucoamylase and use the temperatures the manufacturer recommends if they differ from the rest temperatures associated with the addition of the enzymes in the recipe below.

▸ Makes around 5 gallons (19 liters) of wash

▸ OG: 1.086–1.092 | FG: 1.005–1.011 | ABV: 9.5–11.5%

MAKE THE WASH

1. Add 4 gallons (15 liters) of water to your mash tun heated to boiling, 212°F (100°C).

2. Stir in the yellow corn flakes (and optional hulls) and the hold temperature between 203 and 212°F (95 and 100°C) for 60 minutes.

3. Add 1 gallon of cool water to bring the mash temperature to 149°F (65°C) and stir the Distiller's Malt into the mash tun.

4. Hold the temperature at 149°F (65°C) for 30 minutes.

5. Let the temperature fall to 139°F (59°C) and add the enzymes.

6. Keep the mash temperature between 123 and 139°F (51 and 59°C) for 1 hour.

YOU WILL NEED:

▸ **12 lb. (5.4 kg) Briess Brewers Yellow Corn Flakes**

▸ **12 oz (340 g) rice hulls (optional)**

▸ **3 lb. (1.4 kg) Rahr High DP Distillers Malt**

▸ **12 g Still Spirits Distiller's Glucoamylase Enzyme**

▸ **12 g Still Spirits Distiller's High Temperature Alpha-Amylase Enzyme**

▸ **20 g Still Spirits Whiskey Distiller's Yeast**

▸ **6- to 8-liter medium toast or charred oak barrel, new or used for bourbon (or 100 g medium toast oak chips)**

For a complete list of equipment you'll need, please see pages 11–13.

Make sure all equipment and surfaces have been cleaned and sanitized.

THE GEOGRAPHY OF SPIRITS

Geographic location can really add confusion to the world of spirits. A whiskey, say bourbon whiskey, can be made the same way in Kentucky and Ireland, using 51 percent corn and new charred oak barrels, but in Ireland it would have to be called something other than bourbon whiskey. "Barrel-aged corn whiskey" or "Irish corn whiskey" might end up on the bottle instead. They can call it most anything but bourbon, even if it's made and tastes exactly like a bourbon would. This is because it doesn't meet a geographic designation, origination, or indication. This requirement is meant to uphold tradition and value, meaning certain spirits can be called something only if it's made in a particular place. The United States Congress recognizes bourbon whiskey as a "distinctive product of the United States." In the same way, wines like champagne must be given a different name (like "sparkling white wine") if produced outside the Champagne region of France.

7. Heat 2.7 gallons (10 liters) of sparge water to 180°F (82°C) and sparge grain. Optional: You may choose to bring the wort to a boil to ensure it is free from bacteria prior to fermentation and to condense it down (15 minutes is ample time to ensure a sterile wort, and up to an hour should be ample to condense wort to less than 5 gallons, should space in your fermenter or still be an issue). Neither is required if your equipment is clean and your fermenter is at least 6 gallons (23 liters), large enough to manage around 5.25 gallons of wort.

8. Cool the collected wort and add to the fermenter.

9. Pitch yeast once the temperature is below 95°F (35°C).

10. Ferment at 72°F (22°C) for 14 days. Transfer the wash to your still.

DISTILLING AND AGING

11. Perform a single run with a pot still, collecting only the hearts, or perform a stripping and spirit run for a more delicate flavor and higher-proof aging whiskey.

12. If you'd like more of a moonshine, cut to between 40 and 50 percent and drink clear and unaged. Or age on oak for any amount of time, but I recommend 3 weeks to 3 months at less than 125 proof.

Optional: Instead of using flaked corn, you could also use food-grade cracked corn, cornmeal, or corn grits. Or try substituting flaked or malted wheat for the corn in the recipe to make a wheat whiskey. The same would be true if you substituted flaked or malted rye for the corn to make a rye whiskey.

SO, WHAT'S A "BEER" WHEN YOU'RE DISTILLING?

You may hear (mostly commercial) distillers refer to the beer. In Scotland and other places, a whisky during fermentation is sometimes referred to as beer or "distiller's beer." A beer is, at its core, an undistilled whiskey, the same ones you drink usually with some hops added to bitter it down and keep it from being too sweet. As a distiller, instead of moving a beer out of a fermenter and carbonating it in bottles as a brewery would do, we move it to a still and condense it into a spirit ready to be aged on oak.

CHOOSING A STILL
Chapter 10

The still, the iconic symbol of the distillation process. All that metal, all those cool parts. They can be a backwoods, slapped-together, ugly-as-sin eyesore, or a perfectly polished curvy copper masterpiece. Either can make a great spirit. What you decide to go with is up to you.

If you're like me and want to be able to run white spirits, as well as aged brown spirits, you might follow in my footsteps. For neutral spirits, a copper Still Spirits T500 column is a great choice. It's a forced-reflux design capable of clean, high-proof spirit. As well, the Still Spirits Copper Alembic Dome is all you need for great rums, whiskeys, and other pot-distilled spirits. They both fit on either the Still Spirits Turbo 500 Boiler or the Grainfather G30 brewing system. Most of the recipes in this book were tested on one of these two head units.

If you'd like to get creative, the Boka still design has many plans and users online. Not only will you find designs, diagrams, and parts lists, you'll find a community of users happy to help you build this reflux still head. If you're looking to make a pot still, a simple stovetop water kettle still can be effective for experimenting. A stovetop pressure cooker kettle will have lid clamps and can act as a boiler as well. From there it's just up to you to figure out the best head design, which may just be the pressure cooker lid with copper tubing attached and run to a condenser.

Since there is such a variety of ready-to-purchase stills out there, hopefully the information in this chapter helps you make an informed decision if you intend to buy your still.

TALKING STILLS

Whether you decide to buy or build, you need to understand the four key components of a still:

- The boiler
- The heat source
- The condenser
- The head

From bottom to top, each of these components has a significant effect on your distillation. The heat source needs to be controllable and strong enough to manage your boiler and wash volume. The boiler should be the appropriate shape and size to support the volume of wash and also be appropriately fitted to the head and heat source sizes. The head needs to offer the right amount of reflux for the type of spirit you would like to produce. And the condenser needs to keep up with the vapor your boiler is producing.

When it comes to the head, a "reflux column still," or partially abbreviated as "reflux still" or "column still," is primarily focused on producing pure, clean ethanol. It's a great choice if that's what you're looking for! On the other hand, an "alembic pot still," often just called an "alembic" or "pot still," is domed, usually without a tall column, and with a condenser arm or possibly a "flake stand with worm," a type of condenser that consists of a coil of copper tubing run through a small bucket of cooling condensing water. This method of distilling creates less reflux, less vapor falling back into the still to be redistilled from a dome than in a packed column, and thus allows more congeners and therefore flavor through.

If you're interested in a pot still, I'm guessing that in most cases you're planning on oak aging your spirits, or running the spirit through twice, a stripping and spirit run, as the still is designed to produce a larger number of impurities and congeners that need to age or be redistilled to improve.

Because each is a tool designed for specific goals and purposes, neither still is the best option for every spirit out there. With that in mind, many still boilers can take either a column or a dome, which means you can interchange these two options depending on what sort of spirit you'd like to produce. If you think you're going to be crafty and creative and distill a number of different spirits, finding a boiler that fits both a reflux column and an alembic dome makes sense.

There are a couple options to consider when purchasing a still that go beyond just the style of head (column or dome), so let's look at the heat source, the size and style of the boiler body, and the condenser options before we circle back to the details on the heads.

STILL BODY: THE BOILER AND HEAT SOURCE

The boiler, the body of the still, is a great place to start when deciding what sort of still you'd like. It can actually be the decision that all others are based on. The size of still and heat source you'd like to use can have implications on the type of head unit you go with. Will you be distilling inside or outside? Do you want to make a flask, bottle, jug, or barrel of booze at a time? What will your heat source be? Do you have access to natural gas or electricity where you want to distill? Will you be tied to your stovetop? Maybe you will be running a more portable outdoor rig with a propane burner?

Although they can all look quite different, but also quite simple, a boiler body is typically needed. The boiler of a still will need to seal well because we don't want vapor escaping out—it'll be your alcohol leaving first! Clamps, tape, rye flour paste (equal parts water and rye flour), or even a threaded lid will work. An ordinary kettle can get the job done if it can seal tightly enough to not let precious ethanol vapor escape.

The size of the boiler you use should reflect the amount of finish spirit you'd like. A simple and quick example: If you're running 5 gallons (19 liters) of an 11 percent ABV wash and you collect 1 gallon (4 liters), the highest potential you'd be able to collect would be 55 percent, ideally, condensing all of the alcohol in 5 gallons into 1 gallon. You'll actually collect just under this, probably between 0.75 and 0.95 gallons (3 and 3.5 liters) at 55 percent ABV depending on your still's capability, as some of that alcohol will be in your heads and tails, and you'll leave it behind to be discarded or run again.

If you are charging (filling) your still with 5 gallons (19 liters) of wash I would recommend a minimum of a 6.25 gallon (24 liter) boiler. Although it's not a mathematically determined amount, you'll want around 25 percent of your headspace to be open to account for foam buildup in most still bodies. This buildup happens naturally during the boiling process with most washes. A small amount of foam in your column or condenser will contaminate your spirit's flavor and aroma more than you'd expect. If you get this sort of surging you might notice it as steam coming off your condenser, or "contaminated" spirits coming out. Your spirits should always come out clear.

FOAM CONTROL

Now is a good time to bring up a couple of ways to control foam. Some foaming isn't an issue, but if solids build up at the bottom of your dome or condenser column, they can make the still act strangely and your output sporadic. One way is to fill your boiler only halfway, maybe even less if you're being cautious. You should expect a large amount of foam from high-protein washes, say a mash that started with many distiller's malts (barley) or oats. If you are using a submerged heating element, make sure this doesn't run dry during the run. Also be sure not to have too much solid material in your wash. If you have a lot of solids going into your boiler, this can cause excessive foam and issues if the solids are carried up into your column or dome.

An easy way to control foam, if cutting back your run volume doesn't sound fun, is to add some antifoam or distilling conditioner to the kettle prior to running the still. This is typically food-grade silicone that doesn't allow foam to build on the surface during the boil. It acts as a surfactant, lowering the surface tension.

Lastly, adding ceramic rings (boil enhancers, also known by the brand names Pall or Raschig rings) to the bottom of your kettle may help even out your boil, avoiding foaming issues; the rings break up bubbles forming on the bottom of your kettle that can lead to the more serious issue of steam and wash surging through your still.

What can be used as a boiler? Almost anything that can be securely and tightly closed. Examples include

- Pressure cookers
- Hot water heater boilers
- Teapots
- Kettles with clamps
- Stainless milk canisters
- Electric kettles
- Electric brewing systems
- All-stainless commercial kegs
- Kettles actually designed for distilling
- Alembic copper boiler bodies

If it can be tightly closed and boiled in, with a controlled release of vapor into your still head and then condenser, it can probably be used.

A good boiler fits your still head (keep reading), size requirements, and available heating solution. Electricity can be limiting in terms of boil volume, but it's also one of the most accessible ways to heat a boiler. For that reason, I often use an electric boiler. In my case, it's a Still Spirits Turbo 500 Boiler or the Grainfather G30 brewing system. Both fit the still heads I use and are sized right for the amount of wash I typically ferment. More on the still heads I use later.

Heating your boiler may seem like a no-brainer. You may have only one or two options at your disposal. Even if this is true, there are some details you should consider.

ELECTRIC

You might be thinking of your stovetop, but it goes well beyond this, As mentioned earlier, I often use the Grainfather G30 brewing system. This is a 7.9 gallon (30 liter) electric kettle with a concealed element built in. It's great for a gentle, controlled distillation. It has a voltage controller built in, so I don't need to worry about boiling too fast. It also has enough headroom that I can do a 5 gallon (19 liter) wash without worrying about foam or surge boiling due to overfilling the boiler.

Another option with some portability and control is an electric hot plate. This allows you to use any flat-bottomed boiler, but it may be somewhat limited in power. An immersion heating element can be built right into the still, typically run through the side with the power cord run outside of the body. It might have some voltage control or thermostat to help manage boiler temperature, which is always helpful. Immersion heating elements can be effective, affordable, and easy to change if you have access to the inside of the boiler. It's nice to have your heater built right in, but watch for scorching or burning your element out if your still runs dry, as these typically don't heat from the bottom. An induction electric burner is a safe and easy way to heat a still. An induction burner stays cool while it heats; using an electromagnetic field, it only heats the magnetic metal in the base of the boiler. You'll need an induction-ready boiler body, which can be easily found.

GAS

Using propane or natural gas can give you a much more powerful supply of energy in the form of a direct flame. Burner size and quality does make a difference. An underpowered burner can make your distillation day twice as long. If you're using a tank, running out of fuel can be an issue. If you're thinking of using gas, and planning on instilling a 5-gallon wash, you won't need a burner bigger than 54,000 BTUs. You will want a needle valve or fairly sensitive valve to control your flame. You'll also want a good windscreen as the temperature in your boiler can wildly fluctuate outdoors, especially in the wind. A jet burner or ring burner (sometimes called a banjo burner) can work equally well for distilling if you can keep the flame low enough and have some control over it.

There are other direct heat sources for your boiler, such as a wood fire. Although this is a traditional moonshine method, it's really tricky to control a still over an open fire pit. A lot can go wrong. If you're comfortable trying this method, feel free. But overheating, underheating, cold spots, hot spots, and wear and tear on your still can all be a bit of a hassle.

There are also other indirect heating methods, some of which are used in commercial distilling, such as steam jacketed kettles or double boilers. These make a lot less sense for home distillers as they often rely on a large installed energy source away from the boiler to make it work.

THE BOILER AND CONDENSER RELATIONSHIP

Boilers need to be in tune with the condenser to not produce more vapor than the condenser can manage to cool. You'll see steam coming out of your condenser if your heat source is working too fast for your condenser. The general rule? Any heat added during boiling at the start of the process needs to be equally subtracted during condensing at the end of the process.

Consider the size of the condenser needed to make this happen in relation to your heating source and boiler. For those with a mind for mathematics, science, and engineering, it's possible to determine the ideal condenser size based on the amount of energy you're producing. A condenser a bit larger than you think you need is not a bad idea, as it's easy enough to cut back the cooling power (slow your cooling water source down or warm it up) but can be hard to increase it. The same goes for a burner; it's okay to go with something larger, as long as you can decrease it to a lower output heat.

continued ▶

Generally, you can expect to effectively produce up to 2 ounces (59 milliliters) of distillate every minute with a 1,000-watt heater working at capacity. At 1,500 watts, a pretty common electric kettle boiler size for stills in the United States on 110v power, you'll produce 3.5 ounces (104 milliliters). Again, this is just a general rule of thumb and can depend on the amount of alcohol you began with, as well as how well your still condenses alcohol. If you're producing faster than this and know your heat source is, say, 1,500 watts, then you know you might not be effectively condensing, potentially even losing spirit as vapor.

CONDENSERS

The condenser is possibly the most critical component of a still for many reasons. It's as self-explanatory as it sounds. The condenser unit on a still is designed specifically to condense vapor back to liquid for collecting. If we could collect and drink steam, this wouldn't be necessary, but the actual act of making steam is what allows us to separate the alcohol from the water. Heating a boiler turns liquid to vapor, while a condenser does the opposite. It uses cooling to turn vapor to liquid.

A condenser has the same challenges as boiling in terms of energy use and changing temperature. The temperature differential and the surface area are the two most important factors affecting the condenser efficiency.

COOLING DOWN THE VAPOR

As important as any part of the still, the condenser needs to turn our vapor running through our still back into a liquid for collection purposes. If it doesn't, our alcohol just evaporates off into the atmosphere and all that hard work up until this point was for naught.

Transfer of heat is critical to a condenser working well. That transfer of heat out of the vapor is directly proportional to the amount of area available for the hot vapor to pass through. It's also directly proportional to the difference in temperature between the cooling substance, like water, and the vapor to be cooled. If you double the cooling surface area, you potentially double the heat transfer. If you halve the difference in temperature between the cooling water and the vapor, you halve the heat transfer available. A condenser is designed to maximize the surface area for heat transfer.

CONDENSER MATERIAL

The materials used to make a condenser are very important. Most materials can be measured by their thermal conductivity or resistance. Thermal resistance is how easy or difficult it is for heat to flow through the material (metal in the case of most stills). Since the materials we use to make a condenser form the barrier between the cooling substance (usually water) and the hot vapor (our alcohol) that we want to condense, the inner condenser material is most important.

Copper does not have much resistance and will easily let heat pass through. For this reason it makes an excellent condenser. If we give copper a value of 1, then we can compare other metals that could make up your condenser against copper. After this review, I hope you consider copper first:

MATERIAL	THERMAL RESISTANCE
Copper	1
Aluminum	2
Brass	3
Stainless Steel (321)	27
Glass	490

Aluminum and brass corrode, so these aren't recommended. It is twenty-seven times harder for heat to pass through stainless steel. This is an important design consideration, as stainless steel will require a super cold condenser to work well.

So why do we find stills made of stainless steel and glass if the condenser is so inefficient? Glass gets used in labs because you can see the reactions occurring, and it can be used with a bunch of different fluids, some corrosive. Stainless steel is used because it is cheap and easy, as well as long lasting, and not too difficult to form into still parts like condensers.

CONDENSER DESIGN

If you aren't able to properly condense, vapor can move through undisturbed and escape out of the still! The goal of a condenser is to turn your vapor back into a liquid for collection. A lot of energy was used to create your spirit vapor, and now the same vapor needs a similar amount of energy to return to a liquid. Condenser design plays a crucial role. A large variety can be purchased off the shelf. Some are built into or come with the column or dome head unit as a package. Let's take a look at the common condensers out there.

Air Cooled: Small tabletop stills can effectively use air cooling due to their size. In its simplest form, a large fan condenser is at the top of a boiler and blows cooler air on a coil. Compared to water, it's not very efficient but efficient enough to condense the vapor coming up off a small still, as long as the still heats slowly enough. This same tactic can be taken with a long condenser arm or coil and multiple fans. Energywise, it may never be the most effective way to cool a condenser arm, but it does allow you to not have a multilayered, double-walled, or jacketed condenser arm, as you'd need to effectively use a liquid like water in the following examples.

Liebig Condenser: The simplest and the most popular for home distillers, this style effectively uses water. If you've been looking at home stills, you've probably seen a straight arm angled down coming away from a column or dome. This is the condenser, and it's most likely a Liebig-type condenser. Inside, the hot vapor is condensed down a center tube, and the cold water is circulated through in a jacket around this tube, moving up the arm from an inlet at the bottom to an outlet at the top. Cool water goes in through an outer jacket tube; vapor is enclosed in the inner tube, condensing as it meets the surface it shares with the water, running down the condenser and eventually out to your collection vessel. As simple as that!

Graham condenser (see page 198)

Graham Condenser: So how can we improve on the Liebig design? Create more surface area to be cooled and condensed. One way to achieve this would be to lengthen the straight condenser tube, which might get unwieldy or expensive given time. Or use a Graham condenser and spiral the vapor tubing inside the cooling jacket, allowing the passage through the condenser to be quite long in a shorter continuous space. The condenser and coils should be as vertical as possible to allow the outer shell to fill around the coiled tube. Any angle upward may trap liquid and block your flow of vapor, which could cause some back pressure, or cause the still to "burp" as it releases liquid.

Worm Condenser: If you've seen a condensing coil on a traditional alembic or moonshine still, you'll know what a worm condenser is. It's a coil of copper tubing, a "worm" that comes down vertically from the top of the still and sits in a bath of cold water, called a flake stand or worm tub, and condenses there before moving on to your collection vessel. This is effectively a Graham condenser, just not completely enclosed. The cooling condenser, the flake stand, can simply be a plastic bucket or anything else that can hold a coil of copper tubing. As in the Graham condenser, this should be fairly vertical; the coil should work its way at a slight angle to the bottom of the flake stand before coming out. The flake stand will have an inlet for water at the bottom and an outlet at the top.

Vigreux Condenser: On paper it's essentially a Liebig condenser with its surface area increased by indenting the sides. It's common in labs but less popular in the home-distilling world, unless working on a pretty small scale where lab-sized equipment makes sense.

Shell and Tube Condenser: A type of condenser that's now used across virtually every distillation industry, numerous small tubes carry cold water through a condenser shell that has vapor passing the opposite way. The amount of cold surface area is quite high due to the larger number of cooling tubes running through, making this design quite effective. It's sometimes referred to as the shotgun, firebox, or crossflow condenser.

Coldfinger Condenser: This style can look like the opposite of a Liebig condenser, because the cooling water runs inside instead of outside. It's also typically run into the top of a column, simply a U-shaped dip, or single reservoir to cool and condense the vapor as it rises. It might also be a coil and shows up in some of our still heads later on.

I hope this gives you some idea of how many designs there are for condensers out there, as I've only covered the most popular. Many other designs are based on combinations or variations of the above. The condenser can be a difficult part to build yourself without a bit of thought and machining skills. Look at what's available and see if it makes sense. As mentioned, a condenser often comes with a still head, and we typically base our purchase on the column or dome, not on the condenser, though I encourage you to give both equal consideration. See if there are ways to improve what you've received if improvement is even needed.

So why does vapor find its way to the condenser? Vapor pressure, firstly. It's looking to escape to the atmosphere. Also, hot vapor, like hot air, rises. So, it naturally heads upward in the still until it reaches the top and then the inside of the condenser where it's much cooler than the atmosphere closer to the boiler. Even if your condenser is broken and not providing any cooling, the vapor may still condense on the surface as the path narrows; however, it also may revaporize. A mix of steam and liquid will come pouring out of your condenser without any cooling substance.

One other thing to cover as we finish up with condensers: Running the cooling liquid counter to the hot vapor (soon to be condensed to liquid) is the most efficient and effective cooling method. General rules of thermodynamics say this is the most effective way to cool, and so we will! We want to remember this later on when we discover things like dephlegmators on flute columns or cooling coils inside of reflux columns.

Worm condenser
with Flake Stand

STILL HEAD: COLUMN

Nothing defines a still more than the style of head unit chosen, whether a column or a dome. A reflux still is based around a tall column and is a great option for those making neutral, clear spirits, also called white spirits. These include

- ▶ Vodka or neutral spirit
- ▶ Gin or infused spirits
- ▶ White rum
- ▶ Silver tequila
- ▶ Liqueur bases
- ▶ Spirits for flavoring

Columns can be packed with material, typically copper, stainless, or ceramic rings. In commercial settings, or more expensive home stills, the column may create reflux with horizontal plates or bubble plates inside. Unpacked columns minimize the amount of reflux and can be used for things like bourbons and brandies. We'll talk a bit more about using a reflux still like this; it's a consideration for those of you with a column head already looking to produce aged spirits.

Do neutral and clear spirits sound like what you're most interested in making? Cool! Definitely get yourself a reflux column, because you can't make a good clean neutral spirit or vodka without it. There are numerous types of column designs to consider.

PACKED COLUMN

This is the most basic of reflux columns out there. Simply put, this is a column stuffed with packing that forces the vapor to find its way through small gaps as it rises through the column. It struggles to do so and droplets form as vapor changes back into a liquid at cooler temperatures away from the boiler. This liquid falls, increasing the chances of vapor running into liquid and joining in the cascade of fluid back to the boiler. As the temperature increases in the column, the alcohols at lower boiling points can make their ascent without falling all the way back into the boiler, vaporizing in the column until they reach the top of the column and find their way to the condenser.

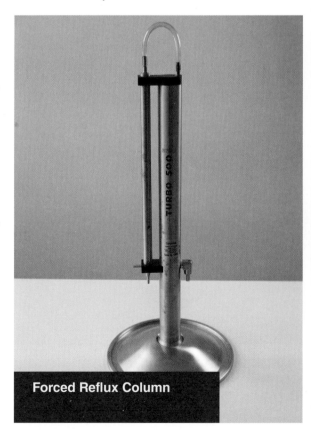

Forced Reflux Column

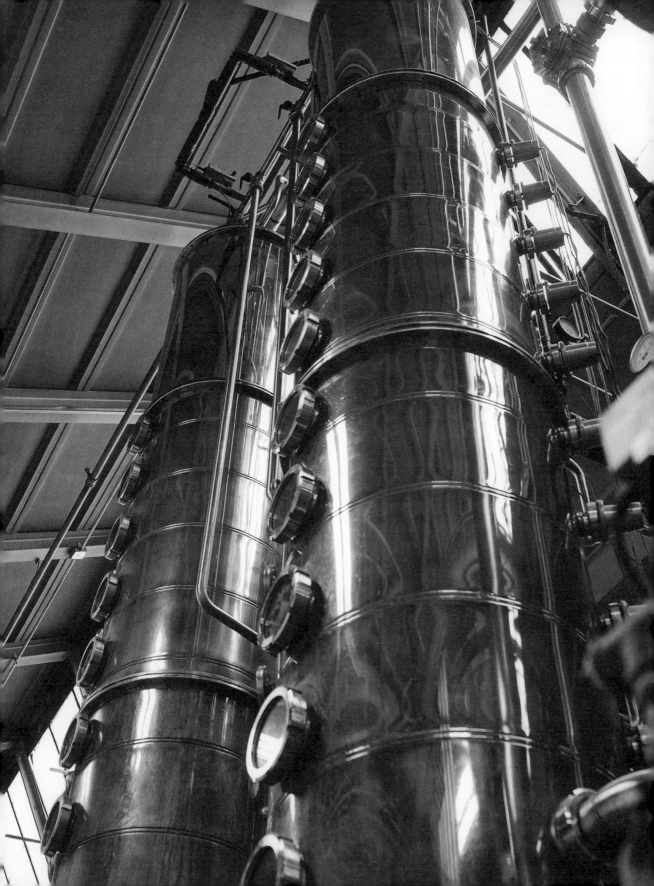

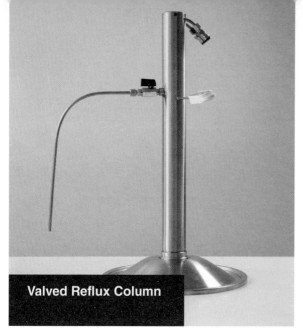

Valved Reflux Column

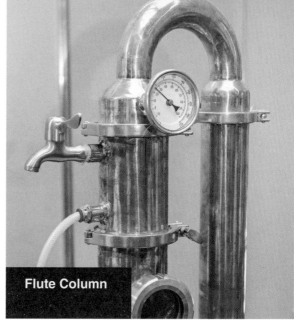

Flute Column

FORCED REFLUX

A packed column may be a part of a more elaborate design, using a cooling coil or line inside the column as well. Typically referred to as a "forced reflux" design, it may also be called a "vapor management" column or still. This is an improvement on a simple packed column as the vapor is forced into a cooler environment at the top of the column, usually coming into contact with the copper coil with cold water running through it.

VALVED REFLUX

A valved reflux is similar to a forced reflux except, as you might have guessed, there's a valve. That valve is used to collect your distillate. It's an all-in-one design that relies on the cooling coil as the condenser inside the column. The still may be packed and/or have slanted plates, which forces some reflux as well as provides a place for liquid to pool inside the column where it can be collected. There are also offset columns, or "external valved reflux" columns, which have a secondary column built off the primary column attached to the boiler. These have a valve below and condensate is easily collected as it pools in the bottom of the offset column. One style of valved reflux column you'll come across is the Boka (also known as Bokakob, or Bok) that's been designed for home distillers.

FLUTE

A flute column is possibly the most complex and commercial-looking column of the bunch. Flute columns are typically segmented and provide plates that create reflux instead of packing. The windows into each segment provide a look at the process as it's happening. They typically either contain bubble plates or perforated plates with downcomers. The point of bubble plates and perforated plates with downcomers is to allow liquid to gather and escape back down to the lower plate. This liquid level creates a barrier for vapor to pass through, which collects and cools new vapor, not allowing the heavier liquids with a higher boiling point to continue up the column. The top contains a dephlegmator, similar to the cooling coil at the top of the column in a forced reflux still, except that its numerous tubes are being cooled by a direct cold-water source or, in some instances, from water being used by the condenser.

Any of these columns will work; it comes down to personal preference. All are potentially capable of 94 percent (188 proof) ABV distillate coming out of your still. A simple packed column would need to be quite tall or well controlled to do so. All are also capable of running a sizable collection of hearts out around 90 percent (180 proof) ABV if designed well. Again, a simple packed column may struggle a bit without some control.

Copper dome still with helmet and an offset column.

STILL HEAD: POT

The alternative to a reflux column on top of your still is a pot, or alembic, dome. To clarify, I hope you're catching on that a still can go by a few different names. If I say alembic, dome, or pot, I mean the same thing: a still without a column, with some sort of attachment that might be round, square, or flat in shape at the top of the boiler. They get used interchangeably these days, just as column still and reflux still do, one and the same.

So, a dome might actually look more like a soft-serve ice cream cone, a helmet, an onion, or just a simple rounded domed or flat lid, but the purpose of each is the same: to create some reflux of the alcohols and congeners, but not so much that the flavor is completely stripped away. Think of a dome as an intentionally less effective column still. It's not a bad thing! It just depends on what you want to do. The clear and aged spirits that can be made on an alembic include:

- Whiskeys, bourbon, and scotch
- White and aged rum
- Aged mezcals (which includes tequila)
- Aged brandies (like cognac)
- Gin (not aged, but run twice)

If you're after darker (brown) aged spirits, then going with an alembic dome is probably a great way to start your dabbling in distilling. Let's look at a few options and designs out there.

Helmet

ONION

Without trying to add to the confusion too much, the term alembic often refers specifically to stills with an onion-shaped head. These are an ancient design, still quite popular, and almost always copper. They can be fitted like a sleeve to the top of a boiler, often needing something like tape or a flour paste to attach to the body. These can also be fitted to a body or lid via a large tri-clamp fitting or similar commercial stainless fitting.

HELMET

I'm segregating this out from the onion head, as it seems the industry has accepted that this typically refers to the inverted version of an onion, with the bulbous part of the still head being at the top. Helmet, though, is often used for nearly any type of pot still head attachment. One interesting thing you'll find is that there is no standard for how to take an inverted onion–type helmet to a condenser. Some folks attach a long empty column; others add a swan neck and lyne arm (see below); others go right to a condenser. Its commercialized production means it's easy to find as a tri-clamp attachment to many stills and lids, and numerous tri-clamp attachments will fit above. Experimentation to find the combination that delivers the flavor you are after is key if you go this route.

Copper dome head with onion

COPPER OR STAINLESS DOME

Simply an inverted bowl, this is a perfectly round lid that fits on top of a round boiler. This dome is a fairly common design to be fitted on standard kettles. Although simple, it is effective enough if paired with the right boiler and condenser. A copper dome will help reduce sulfur compounds, improving the flavor and aroma of your distillate.

COPPER OR STAINLESS LID

A lid that can be closed tightly via a large barrel clamp, or a set of clamps, on a kettle is a type of pot still head. It also often includes a small amount of unpacked column above the lid to connect a condenser. Other times it simply runs out a small piece of tubing directly to a condenser! This might sound quite simplistic—a flat kettle lid with some tubing run out of it—but in the right hands, and with a bit of practice, it will create spirits!

SWAN NECK AND LYNE ARM

Not truly the definition of a type of pot still, these are features that exist in many a still head. A traditional commercial whiskey pot still consists of a cone inverted on a boiler body tapering at the top into a tube that goes to a condenser. This swan neck, connected to the boiler and running to the lyne arm, which connects the swan neck to the condenser, can take many forms. The swan neck can be tall or short and squat, with the lyne arm pointing upward, parallel to the ground, or pointing downward, as you might imagine it. Other still designs incorporate one or both of these features. An alembic, although usually somewhat bulbous and bottom heavy (think onion), often has a lyne arm and a swan neck as well, making it a bit more pear shaped, especially in commercial distilleries.

UNPACKED/UNREFLUXED COLUMN

Most columns you can fill with packing can be used as a pot still. It's key you cut back on the amount of reflux happening in the column. If it's a forced reflux still or flute still, you may want to also consider not running any cool water to your column's cooling coil or dephlegmator, as long as you still have a condenser that can receive cool water and condense. Some columns may have plates that are not removable, like a bottom plate that holds the packing in the column. These will always create some reflux (any obstruction in your column will), but probably not enough to worry about. It's worth considering a reflux column if you think it'll be easy enough to cut down on the reflux, and if you think the majority of your spirits will be neutral or clear.

The tricky part is that all of these pot still attachments will work. It's again going to come down to personal preference. One reason distillers like building their own still is that it adds an artistic touch to what can truly be "six of one, half dozen of the other" type decisions when looking at equipment. I hope this overview of stills and their parts has provided you with some options and suggestions you can use to find the best still for you.

Copper dome head

GLOSSARY

ABV | alcohol by volume. The percentage of liquid that is alcohol.

Acetaldehydes | a congener that is identified by a strong fruit odor and green apple peel flavor. It's produced during fermentation but can also show up when ethanol is oxidized.

Activated Carbon | what spirit is filtered through during polishing. It can also be added to the fermentation for additional removal of impurities created during the ferment.

Alcoholmeter | *see Proof & Tralle Hydrometer*

Alcometer | *see Proof & Tralle Hydrometer*

Adsorption | in spirit polishing, when congener molecules attract and stick inside the porous surface of activated carbon, effectively being removed from the collected spirit.

Alpha-Amylase Enzyme (AA) | a key enzyme that breaks down starch into more simple sugars during mashing.

Agave | typically in reference to the sugary syrup used in distilling that comes from the blue agave plant.

Alembic (Still or Dome) | refers to a rounded copper pot-style stills or a bulbous copper top to a still, often with a lyne arm to a flake stand for condensing.

All-Grain | used in home brewing and home distilling to define the process of brewing primarily with grains and not relying on malt extract or other sugars as the main ingredient for beer or a wash.

Angel's Share | the evaporated spirit lost during aging, particularly barrel aging.

Backset | low ABV wash in your boiler postdistillation.

Bacteria | a small organism that "infects" your fermentation, eating sugars and creating numerous byproducts. It's primary to dunder and can be intentionally used to create unique flavors in whiskies and rums.

Baijiu | typically a clear, light spirit made from rice, and fermented with a mix of mold, yeast, and bacteria called Qu.

Barrel Proof | the higher proof at which most spirit is aged, typically 100 proof or greater.

Beta-amylase Enzyme | a key enzyme in mashing that breaks down maltose (two attached glucose molecules) into separate glucose molecules, a more fermentable sugar.

Blue Agave Spirit | refers to tequila made outside of Mexico.

Boil Enhancers | or boil chips, are used to even out the heat at the bottom of a still's boiler, disrupting potential surge boiling.

Boiler | the part of a still prior to the dome or column of a still that houses the wash and is heated.

Botanicals | any part of a plant that is used to flavor a spirit, typically gin.

Bourbon | a whiskey made in the United States, that must be a minimum of 51% corn.

Brandy | could be any spirit where fruit is the primary source of sugar.

Brew-in-a-Bag (BIAB) | A simple method of mashing that may require only one vessel and a nylon or cotton bag.

Brown Spirits | *see Dark Spirits*

Cachaça | spirit typically made from sugar can juice. Often a light spirit, but it can be aged.

Carbon Dioxide (CO_2) | Gas created by yeast during the absorption of sugar; it's formed along with alcohol during fermentation.

Carbon Filter | Any filter used for polishing spirit with activated carbon.

Cask | *see Barrel*

Cask Strength | *see Barrel Strength*

Cereals | *see Grain*

Cereal Mashing | a mashing technique to convert raw or unmalted grain.

Char | refers to a burnt, blackened surface in a barrel. There are three traditional levels of char.

Cleaner | any detergent used to clean, polish, and remove debris from a surface.

Cold Sparge | a method of sparging that requires less energy than traditional sparging with hot water but may result in rinsing slightly less sugar from your mash.

Collection Vessel | any vessel used to collect spirit during distilling or polishing. This is typically a glass jug or jar.

Column Still | a still designed to provide additional reflux, most often used for light (white) spirits.

Column | a part of the still typically following the boil that provides packing

Condenser | Typically at the end of the still to cool vapor and turn it into spirit for collection.

Congener | additional alcohols and acids that are often considered off flavors in clear spirits but are necessary for flavor development and complexity in aged spirits.

Cooperage | a company that makes barrels, where a cooper, a barrel maker works.

Corn Whiskey | a whiskey made from 80% corn that doesn't need to be aged.

Cuts | also known as fractions, typically refers to the separate portions of spirit taken as they come off the still.

Cut Spirit | spirit that has been diluted.

Dark Spirits | spirit that has been aged, typically on charred or toasted oak, providing the spirit some color.

Dextrose | sugar.

Dextrin | a carbohydrate that is part of starch that contains glucose sugar and must be broken down to smaller glucose units during mashing (sacchrification) to be fermentable.

Diammonium Phosphate | a source of nitrogen for yeast during fermentation, critical to yeast health.

Diastatic Power (DP) | a way to measure enzymatic activity potential of malt. High DP is needed in malt to help convert the starches contained inside and in other grains during the mash.

Distiller's Parrot | a device that collects distillate as it leaves the still and provides a tube that fills and empties where a proof and tralle hydrometer can float and measure the proof of the alcohol inside.

Distilling | a process of separation and purification of liquids through evaporation and condensation.

Dunder | also known as stillage in whiskey making, it's stored in a dunder pit and added during or after fermentation to the fermenter prior to fermentation. When used for whiskey this is referred to as a sour mash.

Enzyme | proteins that create chemical reactions, often during the mash to break starch down into sugar.

Esterification | the change to congeners and complex molecules in the barrel when they come into contact with things like wood and oxygen.

Ethanol | or ethyl alcohol, is the most important part of any spirit, the colorless alcohol we attempt to measure and collect during distillation.

Exogenous Enzyme | external enzymes, typically a powder, that can be added when enzymes from malted grain are not sufficient.

False Bottom | any sort of screen that helps separate wort from grain, typically in the bottom of a mash tun.

Feints | also referred to as the tails, or the third and final part of the run, it may also refer to a mix of the heads (the first part of the run) and tails.

Fermentation (Fermenting) | the process during which yeast convert sugar into alcohol and carbon dioxide.

Fermentation Vessel | a fermentation vessel can be anything that holds your wort, soon to be wash, and in most cases, closes to form an airtight seal.

Filtering | *see Polishing*

Final Gravity | Your second specific gravity reading taken during fermentation and is used to determine your ABV and if your fermentation is complete.

Flake Stand | a type of still condenser that's made up of a vessel that holds a coil (known as the worm) that carries spirit vapor though it. The vessel has cold water recirculated through it that condenses the spirit.

Flour Paste | typically made from rye flour and water to seal a still with loosely joined parts.

Flute | a type of column still.

Foreshots | the first 25–200ml of alcohol collected off a still, potentially containing large amounts of methanol. This portion of the run is usually discarded.

Fractions | *see Cuts*

Free Amino Nitrogen (FAN) | one of the most critical nutrients for yeast, typically provided in malt or yeast nutrient blends.

Fructose | fruit sugar.

Fusel | *see Congener*

Gelatinization | the first step in cereal mashing used to break down raw grains through heat and hydration.

Gin | a spirit containing juniper and other botanicals for flavor and aroma.

Glencairn | *see Nosing Glass*

Glucoamylase Enzyme | a critical enzyme in the breakdown of starch in grain during mashing.

Glucose | the most basic form of sugar.

Grain | a seed from any number of grasses or plants that produce edible seeds that contain starch and can be mashed. The plants that produce grains are often referred to as a cereal.

Gravity | *see Specific Gravity*